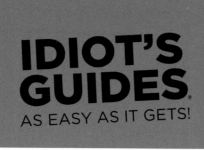

IDIOT'S GUIDES.
AS EASY AS IT GETS!

D0904250

Mediterranean Paleo Cookbook

by Molly Pearl

ALPHA

A member of Penguin Random House LLC

Publisher: Mike Sanders
Associate Publisher: Billy Fields
Senior Acquisitions Editor: Brook Farling
Cover and Book Designer: Becky Batchelor
Development Editor: Kayla Dugger
Production Editor: Jana M. Stefanciosa
Compositor: Ayanna Lacey
Proofreader: Krista Hansing Editorial Services
Indexer: Johnna VanHoose Dinse

First American Edition, 2015
Published in the United States by DK Publishing
6081 E. 82nd Street, Indianapolis, Indiana, 46250

Copyright © 2015 Dorling Kindersley Limited

A Penguin Random House Company

15 16 17 18   10 9 8 7 6 5 4 3 2 1

001-285167-December2015

Published in the United States by Dorling Kindersley Limited.

ISBN: 978-1-61564-861-0

Library of Congress Catalog Card Number: 2015942374

Note: This publication contains the opinions and ideas of its author(s). It is intended to provide helpful and informative material on the subject matter covered. It is sold with the understanding that the author(s) and publisher are not engaged in rendering professional services in the book. If the reader requires personal assistance or advice, a competent professional should be consulted. The author(s) and publisher specifically disclaim any responsibility for any liability, loss, or risk, personal or otherwise, which is incurred as a consequence, directly or indirectly, of the use and application of any of the contents of this book.

Trademarks: All terms mentioned in this book that are known to be or are suspected of being trademarks or service marks have been appropriately capitalized. Alpha Books, DK, and Penguin Random House LLC cannot attest to the accuracy of this information. Use of a term in this book should not be regarded as affecting the validity of any trademark or service mark.

DK books are available at special discounts when purchased in bulk for sales promotions, premiums, fund-raising, or educational use. For details, contact: DK Publishing Special Markets, 345 Hudson Street, New York, New York 10014 or SpecialSales@dk.com.

Printed in the United States

idiotsguides.com

Contents

Introduction

It's easy to find convincing studies or research to support eating one way or another. Around every corner is another outrageous claim that one particular way of eating is the healthiest, with a list of "dos and don'ts" that must be adhered to religiously. While some fad diets roar into the spotlight with sweeping evidence of superiority, some simply stand the test of time, because many of the tenets produce healthy results for a lot of people.

Both the Mediterranean and Paleo diets have been touted as ways to healthier eating. While the Mediterranean diet holds the favor of many within the medical community for its proven heart-health and brain-boosting properties, the Paleo diet has also shown to provide tremendous benefit for reducing systemic inflammation and corresponding conditions. With both sides fighting for dominance in the nutrition world, could there be a way to combine these diets into a lifestyle of eating that's both sustainable in the long term and capable of producing both sets of health benefits? There is.

This book fuses these two diets into one cohesive approach, with a collection of fresh and simple recipes. By focusing on seasonal fruits and vegetables; natural vegetable fats; and plenty of nuts, seeds, and lean protein, the Mediterranean Paleo diet blends both worlds together for a new and delicious way to eat.

Acknowledgments

First and foremost, thanks to my husband, Jason, for the countless hours of recipe writing, testing, food styling, photography, editing, and nutritional analysis. This book would not exist without your encouragement, expertise, and artistic eye.

Thanks to my family in Wisconsin—Mom and Dad, Matt, Sara, Emelia, Ambrose, Estella, and Eleanor. Thanks for teaching me to truly appreciate the food I am nourished with.

Special thanks to Aubrie Weber for helping with recipe formatting, and to Amy Fitzgerald for "falling on the sword" with eggplant recipe testing.

Thanks to Brook, Kayla, Becky, and everyone at Penguin Random House who worked to see this book through to completion.

Special Thanks to the Technical Reviewer

Idiot's Guides: Mediterranean Paleo Cookbook was reviewed by an expert who double-checked the accuracy of what's presented here to help us ensure learning about the Mediterranean Paleo diet is as easy as it gets. Special thanks are extended to Carolyn Doyle.

the mediterranean
Paleo Diet

The word *diet* often conjures images of limited food lists, hunger pangs, and constant cravings for more satisfying foods. The Mediterranean Paleo diet, on the other hand, promotes a huge variety of the freshest fruits and vegetables; hunger-quenching fats; and a vast array of quality meats and responsibly sourced seafood. In this chapter, you find out just what the Mediterranean Paleo diet is, what it can do for your health, and how you can reap the benefits.

What Is the **Mediterranean Paleo Diet?**

The Mediterranean Paleo diet is a **diverse** and **nourishing** way to eat that promotes longstanding **heart, brain,** and **anti-inflammatory** benefits. It supplies a variety of **fruits** and **vegetables; lean proteins** and **fish;** and **plant-based fats, nuts, and seeds.** This long-term lifestyle combines two popular approaches into one plan that can be tailored to your personal needs and goals.

The Mediterranean Diet

Years of research and numerous medical studies have supported the Mediterranean-style diet as an optimally healthy way to eat. However, this approach relies heavily on grains (such as wheat and rice) and legumes (such as beans, lentils, and soy). Most grains are refined in a modern diet and no longer provide the same nutritional benefits as whole-grain versions. Consuming grains and legumes has been linked to an increased inflammatory response that can lead to further digestive and autoimmune problems.

While these foods do provide an important source of complex carbohydrates, similar nutrients can also be consumed through starchy tubers and root vegetables, nuts, and seeds.

STARCHY VEGETABLES/ TUBERS

NUTS/SEEDS

WHOLE GRAINS

FISH/SEAFOOD

POULTRY

BEANS/LEGUMES

FRUIT

LIMITED DAIRY

Eating the Mediterranean Paleo Way

The Mediterranean Paleo diet seamlessly merges the overlapping foods of both plans into one inarguably beneficial approach to eating. The excessive red meat and saturated animal fats of the Paleo diet that can cause long-term heart problems are eliminated, along with the grains and legumes that can cause inflammation on the Mediterranean diet. The primary components then shift to focus on the foods proven to promote long-term benefits—fruits, vegetables, fish, lean proteins, and healthy fats.

High-quality foods are key to this diet approach, so you're encouraged to eat fresh, local, seasonal, chemical-free foods whenever possible. This means looking for quality pasture-raised meats and eggs without additives, antibiotics, or preservatives, and avoiding prepackaged foods that often contain added sugars, stabilizers, or modifiers. This book provides a general guide that can be modified for individual calorie, nutrient, and weight-loss needs, according to what your personal medical professional recommends.

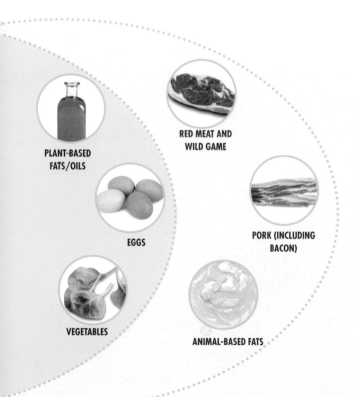

PLANT-BASED FATS/OILS

RED MEAT AND WILD GAME

EGGS

PORK (INCLUDING BACON)

VEGETABLES

ANIMAL-BASED FATS

The Paleo Diet

The Paleo diet relies heavily on animal-based foods. While leaner cuts of meat are emphasized, many who follow this diet consume the majority of their daily calories from meat—including wild game, grass-fed beef, pork and bacon, chicken, and seafood, along with ample amounts of lard and tallow. When you factor in the high price of quality meat, this approach becomes expensive for the consumer. The fact that the Paleo diet also limits or eliminates carbohydrates of all forms (such as whole grains and legumes) makes following the plan difficult in the long term.

Why Should I **Eat This Way?**

Everyone is motivated differently when it comes to dieting. Whether it's for long-term health benefits, weight loss, or relief from inflammatory conditions and allergies, following the components of the Mediterranean Paleo diet can help you meet your personal goals.

A HEALTHIER BODY

Along with moderate daily physical exercise, diets high in fruits and vegetables, nuts and seeds, fish, and olive oil, with minimal dairy and red meat—such as the Mediterranean Paleo diet—have been proven to help prevent type 2 diabetes, heart disease, and stroke. Followers of this eating style have also benefitted from a reduced risk of Alzheimer's disease, dementia, and Parkinson's disease.

REDUCED INFLAMMATION

Inflammation can wreak havoc on major body systems. While it's a primary immune response that's critical to healing, prolonged inflammation may play a part in joint pain, chronic fatigue, obesity, and even cancer. This diet is overflowing with omega-3 fatty acids, fiber-rich vegetables, and dark leafy greens—foods that have been shown to reduce systemic inflammation.

INCREASED ENERGY

Eliminating processed foods can lead to increased energy, as your body no longer has to process and detoxify from these products. Many Paleo diet followers report an increase in focus and concentration—along with a tremendous increase in energy—when consuming cleaner, unrefined, and unprocessed foods. Fresh, ripe, in-season fruits and vegetables are also the most nutrient dense, supplying an immediate source of energy for your body to use.

A LEANER BODY

While diet sodas, nonfat dressings, and low-fat potato chips may seem like waist-reducing choices, they're loaded with refined sugars that can actually have the opposite effect. Refined grains, sugars, and processed oils have been shown to be major factors in weight gain. By eliminating these common offenders, the Mediterranean Paleo diet offers an alternative that is high in fiber and natural plant-based fats that can help you shed extra pounds.

Calorie Intake and Movement

Making the transition to a healthier lifestyle like the Mediterranean Paleo diet requires a shift in thinking. You'll change how you shop for groceries, figure out what recipes you like, and learn what you want to incorporate into your meals.

And if you're looking to lose weight, you'll also have to make changes not only to *what* you eat, but to *how* you eat. Because weight loss has a lot to do with calorie consumption, you have to create a calorie deficit to lose weight, taking in fewer calories than you burn. It's easy to do this with portion control—for example, using smaller plates and then eating only what you put on your plate. You can also use the calorie counts for the recipes in this book to track how much you eat throughout the day.

Along with the food component, the Mediterranean Paleo diet—like every diet plan—should be accompanied by a moderate amount of daily movement. Many studies have shown that gentle exercise at any age can improve overall health and well-being by increasing blood and oxygen flow, strengthening bones, and alleviating stress. While it takes effort to work physical activity into your day, doing so helps your physical and mental health.

Choosing the **Right Foods**

As with any diet change, you set yourself up for **success** by having an understanding of the **appropriate foods** for it, as well as the ones you should **limit** or **avoid.** The following categories can get you started on the right path.

Foods to Eat

The Mediterranean Paleo diet includes a rich variety of foods to get a broad range of nutrients. The images show some great choices to provide the bulk of your dietary intake. Make sure to eat plenty of servings of fruits, vegetables, nuts, seeds, eggs, and olive oil daily. Fish and lean poultry should be consumed at least twice a week.

FRESH, SEASONAL VEGETABLES OF ALL KINDS

NUTS AND SEEDS

EGGS

FISH AND SEAFOOD

LEAN, UNCURED POULTRY

PURE, HIGH-QUALITY OLIVE OIL

RIPE FRUITS

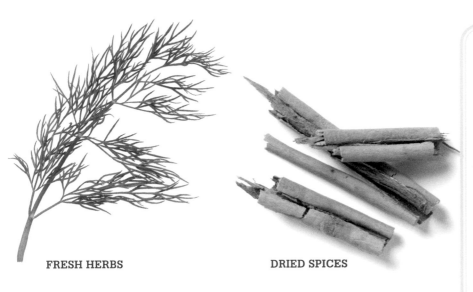

FRESH HERBS

DRIED SPICES

A Note on Red Wine

While a 5-ounce (140g) glass of red wine daily is often an acceptable part of the Mediterranean diet, alcohol of any kind is typically considered a toxin on the Paleo diet. The health effects of alcohol are highly debated within the medical community, but a small amount of alcohol has been shown to reduce the risk of heart disease in some studies. Because of these cardiovascular benefits, it remains on the list of acceptable but limited foods for the Mediterranean Paleo diet.

Foods to Limit

While these foods are allowed on the Mediterranean Paleo diet, they are best consumed in smaller quantities, or on occasion.

Full-fat dairy

Cured meats

Red meat (limit to three to four times per month)

Salt

Honey and natural sweeteners

Animal fats, such as lard, tallow, and ghee

Caffeine

Alcohol

Foods to Avoid

These foods are best avoided while following the Mediterranean Paleo diet. Make sure to look carefully on package labels for any such hidden ingredients.

Refined sugars

Refined grains

Partially hydrogenated oils

Margarine

Additives, modifiers, and chemical preservatives

Poor-quality or highly processed meats and seafood

Legumes, such as beans, lentils, and peanuts

Sourcing Your Ingredients
Responsibly

As fewer people become responsible for providing food for more people, it's important to understand how purchasing choices affect the greater agricultural and environmental communities. Here's a quick guide to making smart grocery choices that help consumers, suppliers, and the environment.

Fruits and Vegetables

Because fruits and vegetables make up so much of the Mediterranean Paleo diet, it's especially important to ask several questions before buying these goods: Has this produce come into contact with chemicals that could transfer to you? How far did it have to travel to get to your table? Is it from a farm that's mindful of sustainable farming practices and fair wages? Is there something else you can use that's local or in season?

While it's difficult and unrealistic to follow all of these practices for every fruit and vegetable purchase, it's possible to keep them in mind while shopping, and to make every responsible choice given the circumstances. Determine what the most important factors are to you, do some local research, and shop accordingly.

Meats

Meat production has a tremendous environmental impact globally. Large-scale meat production is one of the biggest contributors to greenhouse gas emissions; it uses heavy amounts of fossil fuels, water, land, and antibiotics. But meat is also an important part of the food chain and offers many vital nutrients to its consumers. Keeping all of this in mind, it's important to eat meat responsibly. Always look for meat that's antibiotic free, pastured or grass-fed, and humanely raised. Avoid meat that has been injected with brines or sugar water, has added nitrites, or has been highly processed. And as a respectful practice, try to find ways you can incorporate lesser-known cuts or organ meats into your diet to encourage consumption of the entire animal.

Fats and Oils

Extra-virgin olive oil is a staple ingredient for Mediterranean Paleo eaters, so stocking up on a good supply of decent-quality oil will go a long way in the success of these recipes. Many of the cheapest brands are not 100 percent pure pressed olive oil, so make sure to do a little research before heading to the store to see which brands are suitable and available. You may wish to have a more economical olive oil for general cooking and a more flavorful oil to drizzle over salads and fresh vegetables.

Some recipes in this book call for coconut oil. As a saturated fat, it can be a controversial ingredient. However, its ability to act as a dairy substitute is beneficial, so it has been included.

Seafood

As the world population increases, so does the demand for sustainable supplies of seafood. Years of irresponsible fishing and other harvesting practices have destroyed many of the once-thriving ocean and river habitats necessary to support fish populations. The good news is that every region still has seafood resources that are abundant or appropriately farmed. Ask your grocer how they promote sustainable fishing practices, and purchase accordingly. Look for branzino, halibut, North Atlantic shrimp, or yellowfin tuna, and avoid red snapper, orange roughy, and swordfish.

Nuts and Seeds

Nuts and seeds are great resources for healthy omega-3 fats and are a quick and filling way to add extra calories to a plant-based meal. Always look for unsalted nuts to limit sodium intake. To get the most flavor, nuts can be lightly toasted. Simply place nuts in a small pan over medium low heat, stirring constantly, for 3 to 5 minutes, or until fragrant. Once toasted, remove nuts from the hot pan to cool completely before storing them in an airtight container.

Seasonal and Local

To be the most responsible consumer, learn what's seasonally available and local. These products are often the highest in nutritional value because they are fresh and don't waste time, money, and nonrenewable resources in long transport. They are also often the most economical choices because they are widely available during the "on" season. An easy way to learn what's currently in season is to shop at a local farmer's market and take note of what fruits and vegetables are available to purchase at certain times throughout the growing year. However, keep in mind this will vary from region to region.

planning
ahead

There's no better way to succeed with a new diet than to plan ahead! This chapter goes over common variations and substitutions, frequently used spices and mixtures, and essential cooking equipment. It also includes two seasonal meal plans with shopping lists to guide you.

Variations and **Substitutions**

For success on long-term diets like the Mediterranean Paleo diet, nutritionists recommend an 80/20 rule, with strict adherence 80 percent of the time, and the remaining 20 percent allowing variations or substitutions. These are some common variations to cover that 20 percent that may help you stay on track.

Dairy

Dairy is a controversial food for some. If you're lactose intolerant, it should be avoided. If not, you may wish to consume small amounts of full-fat, quality dairy products, such at yogurt, kefir, butter, and cheese. Always look for products from antibiotic-free, pastured, and grass-fed cows, sheep, or goats. The probiotics found in cultured yogurt, kefir, and some fresh curd cheeses are extremely beneficial for the bacteria in your intestinal tract.

In most recipes, coconut oil can be substituted for butter, and coconut milk can be substituted for cream, as indicated in ingredients lists. A recipe for coconut milk yogurt is also included for those who wish to eliminate dairy completely.

Red Meat

While red meat is still encouraged on the Mediterranean Paleo diet, it's restricted to three to four servings per month to stay in step with the amounts used in Mediterranean diet heart-health studies. If you find your blood pressure and cholesterol remain at healthy levels, you may wish to increase your red meat consumption. If not, you can get plenty of iron daily from dark, leafy greens.

Breads and Pastas

Many breads and pastas are made with refined and highly processed grains. They also contain gluten, a controversial protein that can be extremely hazardous for those who suffer from celiac disease and other inflammatory digestive ailments.

As an alternative way to eliminate these processed grains and gluten, this book provides a chapter of recipes using vegetable-based pastas. It also includes several recipes for breads, crêpes, and cakes that offer an alternative for those who wish to eliminate these products 100 percent of the time.

For those who have no adverse reaction to standard bread, you may find that simply moderating portion sizes allows you to keep sprouted and whole-grain versions in your diet on occasion.

VEGETABLE PASTA
A great alternative to traditional processed-grain pastas.

Whole Grains and Legumes

Some may question why whole grains and legumes aren't a huge part of the Mediterranean Paleo diet. While the Mediterranean diet embraces them wholeheartedly, the Paleo diet decidedly does not.

Whole grains and legumes can be an extremely economical source for protein, carbohydrates, fiber, and other essential nutrients. But some skeptics question the ability of our guts to fully absorb and digest these nutrients without sprouting or fermenting first, leading to a fairly strong inflammatory response. Legumes are also a high-carbohydrate source of protein.

For these reasons, whole grains and legumes aren't included in any of the recipes in this book. If you find they fit with your economical or nutritional needs, feel free to include them in moderation as part of your diet.

Special Diets

As with all diets, you have certain allowances for special conditions. Some people require low-glycemic, high-fiber, or gluten-free diets. Athletes and nursing mothers have higher caloric needs than kids or those with a more sedentary lifestyle, and some people have particular allergies to certain foods. To cater to different needs, all of the recipes in this book are cane sugar free, and wheat and gluten free; many are also low carb, dairy free, vegan, or vegetarian. Seek the advice of a medical professional for your individual diet needs.

What About Pork?

For this book, pork is used sparingly. Bacon, ham, and sausage are high in saturated fat and often contain sugar as part of the curing or processing. These meats do add a distinct flavor, however, so enjoy them in moderation.

Herbs and **Spices**

Fresh herbs and spices make a world of difference in simple recipes. From the distinct flavor of fresh basil to the complex aroma of ras el hanout, these additions can make any dish shine. While herbs are delicious fresh or dried, try to use fresh herbs whenever possible to get the most antioxidants and inflammation-reducing effects.

Common Mediterranean Herbs and Spices

While some of the spices in this book may be unfamiliar to you, most can be easily found in the bulk spice section of a grocery store. For easy cooking, stock up on some of these dried essentials. Some come in whole or ground versions, so be sure to check the recipe to get the right kind.

Allspice	Cumin	Rosemary
Basil	Fennel	Saffron
Bay leaves	Ginger	Sage
Cardamom	Marjoram	Sumac
Cayenne	Nutmeg	Tarragon
Chives	Oregano	Thyme
Cinnamon	Paprika (sweet	Turmeric
Clove	and smoked)	
Coriander	Parsley	

Turning Spices into Marinades

It's easy to make quick marinades out of your favorite spices. For 1 pound (450g) meat or sliced vegetables, use 2 teaspoons ground spices (or a mixture of spices) and 2 tablespoons extra-virgin olive oil in a shallow container or resealable bag. Refrigerate while marinating for 2 to 24 hours. Because salt in marinades can make meat and vegetables soggy, wait to season until you're ready to cook.

SUMAC
This dried and ground fruit has a tart flavor that goes quite well with yogurt and lemon.

SAFFRON
This luxurious spice comes from a crocus flower and gives foods a very distinct golden hue.

TURMERIC
This rich yellow powder is made from dried rhizomes and has many health benefits, such as heartburn relief.

PAPRIKA
This crimson spice is made from ground chili peppers and can be smoked or sweet in flavor.

Mediterranean Spice Blends

The following are two common Mediterranean spice blends used often in this book. You can purchase them at any specialty or online store.

Ras el hanout: This North African spice mixture contains an assortment of spices, often including cumin, clove, cinnamon, paprika, turmeric, cardamom, coriander, ginger, allspice, and black pepper.

Za'atar: This blend of spices often is used as a condiment and includes sesame, sumac, salt, thyme, oregano, and marjoram.

Salt

Salt gets a bad reputation for increasing blood pressure and leading to heart stress. While too much salt may have this effect, too little salt can also be detrimental. Natural sea salt (or sodium) is an essential electrolyte that can help with hydration. When consumed in moderation—around 1 to 2 teaspoons in total per day—it has been shown to be a beneficial and necessary part of a healthy diet.

Cooking with Fresh Herbs and Spices

Are you new to cooking with herbs and spices, or simply looking for new ways to cook with them? Here are some extra hints and tips:

- For the most flavor, **add dried herbs and spices at the beginning of cooking,** and leave fresh herbs for the end.

- Remember to **remove bay leaves, whole cinnamon sticks, allspice,** or **cloves** before serving.

- **Saffron stems are best when "bloomed"** in a tablespoon of warm water 5 to 20 minutes before being added (along with the residual water) to a recipe.

- Dried herbs and spices lose vibrancy and flavor on the shelf, and are **best if used within 6 months of purchase.**

Excellent with ripe tomatoes

Try with grilled shrimp

BASIL
This pungent fresh herb has many varieties worldwide, with flavors ranging from sweet anise to lemon.

CARDAMOM
This warm and aromatic spice can be purchased ground or as small green pods full of whole seeds.

TARRAGON
Sold fresh or dried, this slender-leaf herb has a unique flavor and is often paired with chicken and fish.

CORIANDER
The dried seeds of the cilantro plant have a citrus flavor when ground and contain a significant amount of dietary fiber.

Spring and Summer
Meal Plan and Shopping List

BASED ON 2
ADULTS

	BREAKFAST	LUNCH	SNACK	DINNER	PREP
SUNDAY	Asparagus and Spring Mushroom Omelet	Fig and Arugula Salad	Red pepper slices; almonds	Sole with Fresh Tomato Salad	Make Apricot and Pistachio Scones and Mojo Verde
MONDAY	Apricot and Pistachio Scones	Hemp Tabbouleh	Grilled Vegetables with Mojo Verde	Carrot Spirals with Carrot Top Pesto	
TUESDAY	Shrimp and Harissa Frittata	Leftover Carrot Spirals with Carrot Top Pesto	Leftover Grilled Vegetables with Mojo Verde	Bouillabaisse	Make Gazpacho; begin Coconut Yogurt
WEDNESDAY	Leftover Apricot and Pistachio Scones	Leftover Hemp Tabbouleh	Gazpacho	Chicken Tagine with Apricots and Green Olives	
THURSDAY	Olive Oil–Fried Eggs; fresh strawberries	Leftover Chicken Tagine with Apricots and Green Olives	Leftover Gazpacho	Beef Kofta with Pine Nuts and Sumac; Balsamic Cucumbers with Dill	Make Nut and Seed Crackers and Olive and Preserved Lemon Tapenade
FRIDAY	Coconut Yogurt with Fresh Fruit	Leftover Beef Kofta with Pine Nuts and Sumac; Balsamic Cucumbers with Dill	Nut and Seed Crackers; Olive and Preserved Lemon Tapenade	Classic Greek Salad	Marinate chicken for Citrus Grilled Chicken with Greens
SATURDAY	Paleo Crêpes with Lemon Curd	Citrus Grilled Chicken with Greens	Leftover Nut and Seed Crackers; Olive and Preserved Lemon Tapenade	Tuna Steak with Orange and Fennel Salad	

This meal plan provides one week of recipes using fresh spring and summer ingredients, with a shopping list of everything you'll need to make them.

VEGETABLES AND FRESH HERBS

¼ cup fresh oregano
¼ cup fresh tarragon
1 cup plus 2 TB. fresh basil
2 cups flat-leaf parsley
2 TB. plus 1 tsp. fresh dill weed
½ cup fresh mint
1¼ cup fresh cilantro
3 thyme sprigs
12 cups baby arugula (or use baby spinach)
1 small bunch frisee
1 large head romaine
1¼ lb. (575g) small to medium fennel bulbs
8 medium seasonal mushrooms
6 large cremini or white button mushrooms
¾ lb. (340g) asparagus spears
1½ lb. (680g) medium carrots (with greens)
4 medium red bell peppers
2 medium yellow bell peppers
1 jalapeño
2½ lb. (1.25kg) ripe heirloom or large tomatoes
4 medium tomatoes
14 cherry tomatoes
2 small Persian cucumbers
2 large English cucumbers
2 medium zucchini
1 medium head cauliflower
1 (2-in.; 5cm) fresh ginger root
4 small to medium leeks
1 small red onion
2 medium yellow onions
24 cloves garlic

SEAFOOD, MEATS, AND EGGS

19 large eggs
2 (4-oz.; 110g) sole filets
2 (4-oz.; 110g) tuna steaks
½ lb. (225g) halibut, cod, or another firm whitefish
½ lb. (225g) live mussels
1 lb. (450g) live small Manila or steamer clams
4 fresh scallops
¾ lb. (340g) 16- to 20-ct. (about 15) raw shrimp
2 to 3 small anchovy fillets
1½ lb. (680g) boneless, skinless chicken breasts
½ lb. (225g) boneless, skinless chicken thighs
1 lb. (450g) lean ground beef

FRUITS

4 fresh figs (or use 8 dried)
10 oz. (285g) fresh strawberries
2 medium oranges
1 medium lime
11 small lemons
5 oz. (140g) fresh fruit of choice
1½ cup dried apricots

NUTS AND SEEDS

⅓ cup whole pecans
1¾ cups whole almonds
½ cup blanched almonds
½ cup shelled pistachios
1¼ cups hazelnuts
6 TB. toasted pine nuts
½ cup raw sunflower seeds
¾ cup raw pumpkin seeds
1½ cups raw shelled hemp seeds
¼ cup flaxseeds
2 TB. chia seeds
2 TB. toasted sesame seeds
2 tsp. whole caraway seeds
½ cup nuts of choice

SPICES

Sea salt
Freshly ground black pepper
1 bay leaf
Ground cardamom
Cayenne pepper
Ground cinnamon
Ground cumin
Ground ginger
Freshly grated nutmeg
Smoked paprika (optional)
Crushed red pepper flakes
12 saffron threads
Sumac
Turmeric

DRY GOODS

1 qt. (1L) extra-virgin olive oil
10 TB. coconut oil or butter
¼ cup balsamic vinegar
3 TB. sherry vinegar
1 tsp. harissa
1 tsp. hot sauce (optional)
½ cup pitted Castelvetrano olives
½ cup pitted green olives
2 cups pitted green or black olives
1 cup pitted kalamata olives
2 preserved lemons (about 3 TB. sliced rinds)
¼ cup sun-dried tomatoes
⅓ cup artichoke hearts
2 TB. coconut flour
3 cups almond flour
1 cup tapioca flour
1 tsp. baking soda
¾ cup raw honey
5 (14-fl.-oz.; 400ml) cans full-fat coconut milk
2 probiotic acidophilus bifida gel capsules
28 oz. (850g) canned, diced tomatoes
2 qt. (2l) fish or vegetable stock
½ cup (4 fl. oz.; 120ml) chicken stock
½ cup tomato juice
½ tsp. Dijon mustard
1 tsp. whole-grain mustard

DAIRY

2 TB. chevre (optional)
½ cup crumbled feta cheese (optional)
14 TB. unsalted grass-fed butter (optional)

Fall and Winter Meal Plan and Shopping List

	BREAKFAST	LUNCH	SNACK	DINNER	PREP
SUNDAY	Zucchini-Date Breakfast Bread	Cauliflower, Celery, and Bell Pepper Salad with Tzatziki	Dried apricots; almonds	Garlic Ginger Prawns with Spiced Carrot-Currant Salad	Make dressing and seed pomegranate for Pomegranate and Fresh Herb Salad
MONDAY	Leftover Zucchini-Date Breakfast Bread for Paleo French Toast; fresh berries	Pomegranate and Fresh Herb Salad	Leftover Cauliflower, Celery, and Bell Pepper Salad with Tzatziki	Sweet Potato Pasta with Tomatoes and Meatballs	
TUESDAY	Tortilla Espagnole	Leftover Sweet Potato Pasta with Tomatoes and Meatballs	Fresh fruit; pecans	Soup alla Canavese; Olive and Onion Focaccia	Make Bay Shrimp Cocktail Salad
WEDNESDAY	Leftover Tortilla Espagnole	Leftover Soup alla Canavese; Olive and Onion Focaccia	Bay Shrimp Cocktail Salad	Salmon with Butternut Squash Couscous	Make Beet and Carrot Slaw; hard boil, chill, and peel 4 eggs
THURSDAY	Spiced Almond and Orange Porridge	Beet and Carrot Slaw with Tahini and Za'atar; hard-boiled eggs	Leftover Bay Shrimp Cocktail Salad	Paprika-Rubbed Chicken with Broccolini	Make Green Zhug
FRIDAY	Leftover Spiced Almond and Orange Porridge	Leftover Paprika-Rubbed Chicken with Broccolini	Grain-Free Flatbread; Green Zhug	Cauliflower Steaks with Ras el Hanout; Roasted Carrots with Cumin and Yogurt	Make 2 extra Grain-Free Flatbreads to use in Fattoush
SATURDAY	Shakshuka	Fattoush	Leftover Green Zhug; vegetable slices	Coriander-Crusted Beef with Olive-Nut Tapenade; Braised Chard	

This meal plan provides one week of recipes using fresh fall and winter ingredients, with a shopping list of everything you'll need to make them.

VEGETABLES AND FRESH HERBS

4 bunches fresh cilantro
¾ cup plus 1 TB. fresh mint
2 TB. fresh basil
2 TB. fresh basil, parsley, or dill
¼ cup flat-leaf parsley
½ cup fresh oregano
1 tsp. fresh rosemary
4 cups baby arugula
6 leaves lacinato kale
1 lb. (450g) Swiss chard
1 head romaine
2 medium zucchini
3 large heads cauliflower
¾ lb. (340g) broccolini
2 medium radishes
5 large celery stalks
2 red bell peppers
1 yellow bell pepper
2 green Anaheim or jalapeño peppers
2 to 6 green serrano chiles
10 cherry tomatoes
1 medium tomato
2 small cucumbers
2 medium beets (with greens)
2½ lb. (1.25kg) small carrots
11 medium carrots
2 medium sweet potatoes
2 lb. (1kg) celery root
4 medium cremini or white button mushrooms
1 (2-lb.; 1kg) butternut squash
1 (3-in.; 7.5cm) fresh ginger root
1 small shallot
4 green onions
1 medium red onion
5 medium yellow onions
32 cloves garlic
2 cups vegetable slices of choice

FRUITS

4 medium bananas
1 pomegranate
1 medium orange
4 medium lemons
1 cup fresh berries
2 pieces fresh fruit of choice
4 large Medjool dates
1 cup dried apricots
½ cup dried currants

SEAFOOD, MEATS, AND EGGS

24 large eggs
¾ lb. (340g) 16- to 20-ct. (about 16) raw prawns
1 lb. (450g) cooked bay shrimp
2 (6-oz.; 170g) boneless salmon fillet slices
1 lb. (450g) ground chicken or turkey
2 whole chicken legs (1½ lb.; 680g each)
2 oz. (55g) pancetta or bacon
5-lb. (2.25k) beef chuck or shoulder roast

DAIRY

20 oz. (550g) full-fat Greek yogurt or coconut yogurt
1 TB. unsalted grass-fed butter (optional)
2 oz. (55g) Parmigiano Reggiano cheese (optional)
¼ cup crumbled feta cheese (optional)

NUTS AND SEEDS

½ cup walnuts
½ cup whole almonds
¾ cup toasted hazelnuts
2 cups shelled pistachios
1 cup pecans
2 TB. whole flaxseeds
2 TB. chia seeds
1 TB. toasted sesame seeds
½ cup raw nuts of choice

SPICES

Sea salt
Freshly ground black pepper
1 bay leaf
Ground cardamom
Cayenne pepper
Ground cloves
Whole coriander seeds
Ground cumin
Whole cumin seeds
Granulated garlic
Ground ginger
Italian seasoning
Onion flakes
Smoked paprika
Pumpkin pie spice
Ras el hanout
Red pepper flakes
Dried sage
Sumac
Za'atar

DRY GOODS

1 qt. (1L) extra-virgin olive oil
4 cups almond flour
¼ cup coconut flour
1½ cups tapioca flour
2 tsp. baking soda
¼ cup raw honey
2 tsp. apple cider vinegar
1 TB. red wine vinegar
2 (14-fl.-oz.; 400ml) cans full-fat coconut milk
1 tsp. pure vanilla extract
¼ cup coconut oil
1¼ cups pitted kalamata olives
1½ cups pitted green olives
½ preserved lemon (1 TB. sliced rind)
¼ cup roasted red bell peppers
1 (28-oz.; 800g) can diced tomatoes
1 (28-oz.; 800g) can crushed tomatoes
3 TB. tomato paste
5 cups chicken stock
1 cup beef stock (optional)
3 TB. tahini
1 tsp. whole-grain mustard

breakfasts

What better way to start the day than with a Mediterranean Paleo meal? These recipes are packed full of natural vegetable fats, extra greens, and lean proteins. Whether you prefer a savory or sweet breakfast, you'll find options to suit your style.

And because breakfast isn't always the best time to cook, you can even make many of these recipes ahead of time for quick eating on the go.

Fiery harissa, tamed with juicy ripe tomatoes and succulent shrimp, pairs perfectly with a slightly bitter frisée salad in this breakfast frittata.

Shrimp and Harissa
Frittata

 1 FRITTATA   **10 MINUTES**   **30 MINUTES**   **½ FRITTATA**

INGREDIENTS

3 large eggs

1 tsp. harissa

2 TB. fresh flat-leaf parsley, chopped

¼ tsp. freshly ground black pepper

2 TB. extra-virgin olive oil (or 1 TB. unsalted butter and 1 TB. extra-virgin olive oil)

3 small garlic cloves, thinly sliced

¼ cup yellow onion, finely diced

¼ lb. (115g) 31- to 40-ct. (about 8) raw shrimp, shelled, deveined, and roughly chopped

6 cherry tomatoes, quartered

1 small bunch frisée, chopped (about 3 cups)

Juice of ½ medium lemon (about 1 TB.)

Pinch sea salt (optional)

METHOD

1 Adjust the top oven rack to be on the second shelf from the top position (make sure there's enough room above to fit a cast-iron skillet). Preheat the oven to 350°F (180°C).

2 In a small bowl, whisk together eggs, harissa, flat-leaf parsley, and black pepper. Set aside.

3 Heat a 6-inch (15.25cm) cast-iron skillet or ovenproof skillet over medium-high heat. When the skillet is hot, add 1 tablespoon extra-virgin olive oil and wait 30 seconds.

4 Add garlic and yellow onion to the hot skillet and sauté, stirring frequently, for 2 minutes, or until onion is slightly translucent.

5 Add shrimp and cook, stirring frequently, until opaque and a bright pinkish-orange (about 30 seconds). Add cherry tomatoes and cook for another 30 seconds. Remove from heat.

6 Pour egg mixture evenly over top. Place the skillet on the top rack of the oven.

7 Bake for 20 to 25 minutes, or until egg is set in the middle and a toothpick inserted in the center comes out clean.

8 Meanwhile, in a medium salad bowl, toss together frisée, remaining 1 tablespoon extra-virgin olive oil, and lemon juice. Add a pinch of sea salt and freshly ground black pepper, if desired. Divide onto plates.

9 Serve frittata warm or at room temperature with a side of dressed frisée.

EACH SERVING HAS:

Calories 319	Total Fat 23g	Carbohydrate 7g	Protein 22g

Velvety eggs are poached in a **fragrant hot pepper** and **tomato sauce,** and topped with **tangy feta crumbles** and **cilantro.**

Shakshuka

 4 EGGS AND 4 CUPS SAUCE   15 MINUTES   1 HOUR, 5 MINUTES   1 EGG AND 1 CUP SAUCE

INGREDIENTS

- 2 TB. extra-virgin olive oil
- 1 medium yellow onion, diced
- 3 garlic cloves, sliced
- 1 medium red or yellow bell pepper, seeded and diced
- 2 green Anaheim or jalapeño peppers, seeded and diced
- 1 (28-oz.; 800g) can crushed tomatoes, with juice
- 1 tsp. paprika
- ½ tsp. cayenne pepper
- ½ tsp. ground cumin
- ½ tsp. turmeric
- 2 tsp. sea salt
- 2 cups Swiss chard, kale, or spinach greens, roughly chopped
- 4 large eggs
- ¼ cup fresh cilantro, chopped
- ¼ cup crumbled feta cheese (optional)

METHOD

1 Heat a 3-quart (3L) Dutch oven or covered braiser over medium-high heat. When the Dutch oven is hot, add extra-virgin olive oil and wait 30 seconds.

2 Add yellow onion and garlic, and sauté, stirring frequently, for 3 to 5 minutes, or until onion is translucent.

3 Add red bell pepper and Anaheim peppers. Stir and cook for 3 minutes.

4 Add tomatoes (with juice), paprika, cayenne pepper, cumin, turmeric, sea salt, and Swiss chard. Stir with a wooden spoon until combined.

5 Cover, reduce heat to low, and continue to cook, stirring occasionally, for 30 minutes. Taste and add more sea salt, if desired.

6 Break each egg into a small glass bowl. Using a wooden spoon or ladle, carefully make 4 indentations in tomato-and-pepper mixture.

7 Slide each egg out of the bowl into an indentation. Cover immediately and cook for 18 to 20 minutes, or until eggs are cooked to desired doneness.

8 Garnish with cilantro and feta cheese (if using) to serve.

Variation: This is a great recipe to use up any leftover cooked meat you might have on hand; chopped beef, lamb, or chorizo would all be excellent additions.

EACH SERVING HAS:

Calories **223**   Total Fat **14g**   Carbohydrate **16g**   Protein **11g**

This **light and fluffy omelet** is overflowing with **creamy leeks, earthy mushrooms,** and the **sweet anise flavor of fresh tarragon.**

Asparagus and Spring Mushroom Omelet

 1 OMELET   **5 MINUTES**   **15 MINUTES**   **1 OMELET**

INGREDIENTS

- 3 large eggs
- 2 tsp. water
- ¼ tsp. sea salt
- ⅛ tsp. freshly ground black pepper
- 2 TB. extra-virgin olive oil (or 1 TB. extra-virgin olive oil and 1 TB. unsalted butter)
- 1 small leek, white and light green parts only, thinly sliced
- 4 medium fresh mushrooms (any local variety)
- ¼ lb. (115g) asparagus, trimmed and sliced
- 2 TB. fresh tarragon, chopped

METHOD

1 In a medium bowl, whisk together eggs, water, sea salt, and black pepper for about 30 seconds, or until fully combined and slightly foamy. Set aside.

2 Place a medium nonstick skillet over medium-high heat. Wait 30 seconds and add 1 tablespoon extra-virgin olive oil.

3 Add leek and mushrooms to hot oil. Sauté, stirring frequently, for 3 to 4 minutes, or until mushrooms soften and leek slices become translucent.

4 Add asparagus and continue to cook, stirring frequently, for 3 to 5 minutes, or until asparagus is bright green and slightly tender. Remove vegetables from the skillet and set aside.

5 Reheat the skillet over medium heat. Add remaining 1 tablespoon extra-virgin olive oil.

6 When the skillet is hot, pour egg mixture into it. Shake the skillet vigorously to spread egg evenly along the bottom.

7 As egg mixture begins to set up, use a rubber scraper to carefully lift cooked edges from the sides of the skillet. Tilt the skillet to allow raw egg to run down lifted edges toward the bottom of the skillet to cook.

8 When egg mixture is firm but still moist, place sautéed vegetables and fresh tarragon on one half. Using a wide plastic spatula, flip empty half of egg over top of vegetables. Cook for 1 minute, and slide onto a plate. Serve immediately.

Variation: In the fall, replace asparagus with 1 small fennel bulb, sliced, and use chanterelle mushrooms to make a seasonally appropriate **Fennel and Chanterelle Omelet.**

EACH SERVING HAS:

Calories **507**   Total Fat **44g**   Carbohydrate **8g**   Protein **23g**

Classic fried eggs get a makeover with the exceptionally **fruity taste of high-quality olive oil** and are served over a bed of **peppery greens.**

Olive Oil–**Fried Eggs**

 2 EGGS 5 MINUTES 5 MINUTES 1 EGG

INGREDIENTS

2 cups baby arugula or baby spinach

Juice of ½ lemon (about 1 TB.)

4 TB. high-quality extra-virgin olive oil

2 large eggs

¼ tsp. sea salt

⅛ tsp. freshly ground black pepper

METHOD

1 In a medium bowl, toss baby arugula with lemon juice until fully coated. Set aside.

2 Heat a medium nonstick skillet over medium heat. Add extra-virgin olive oil and wait 30 seconds.

3 When oil is hot, crack each egg into the skillet. Sprinkle with sea salt and black pepper, and cook for 30 to 45 seconds, or until egg white is almost completely set.

4 Using a wide spatula, carefully flip over each egg in the skillet. Cook for 15 seconds to 1 minute, or until eggs reach desired doneness. Remove from heat.

5 Divide greens onto small plates. Top each with fried egg to serve.

While any extra-virgin olive oil will do, this recipe shines with an exceptionally flavored oil. For the purest flavor, make sure your bottle is fresh (purchased less than 9 months ago) and has been cold-pressed.

EACH SERVING HAS:

Calories **260**   Total Fat **26g**   Carbohydrate **3g**   Protein **7g**

This classic breakfast tortilla, brimming with **tender celery root slices,** is cooked in a base of **paprika-scented eggs** and garnished with **savory scallions.**

Tortilla Espagnole

| 1 TORTILLA | 15 MINUTES | 45 MINUTES | ¼ TORTILLA |

INGREDIENTS

¼ cup extra-virgin olive oil

1 medium yellow onion, thinly sliced

2 garlic cloves, minced

1 lb. (450g) celery root, peeled and cut into 1- to 2mm slices

1 tsp. sea salt

¼ tsp. freshly ground black pepper

½ tsp. smoked paprika

8 large eggs, beaten

2 scallions, white and light green parts only, thinly sliced

METHOD

1 Heat a 10- to 12-inch (25- to 30cm) cast-iron or ovenproof skillet over medium heat. When the skillet is hot, add extra-virgin olive oil and wait 30 seconds.

2 Add yellow onion and garlic to the hot skillet and sauté, stirring frequently, for 3 to 5 minutes, or until onion softens and becomes translucent.

3 Add celery root, sea salt, black pepper, and smoked paprika to the skillet, and stir with a wooden spoon. Continue to cook, stirring every 5 minutes, for 15 to 20 minutes, or until celery root is tender when pierced with a fork. Taste and add more sea salt, if desired.

4 Spread celery root and onion evenly on the bottom of the skillet. Pour beaten eggs over top of vegetable mixture and cook for about 1 minute. Reduce heat to low and continue to cook for 15 minutes, or until eggs are mostly set.

5 While eggs are cooking, turn the oven broiler on high. Once eggs are mostly set, place the skillet on the highest shelf in the oven. Broil for 5 minutes, or until eggs are completely set and tortilla is golden brown on top.

6 Serve warm, at room temperature, or chilled with sliced scallions on top.

Variation: To make a **Chorizo and Piquillo Pepper Tortilla,** cook ¼ pound (115g) ground chorizo along with onion, and add 3 thinly sliced piquillo peppers to vegetables after cooking.

EACH SERVING HAS:

Calories **338**   Total Fat **24g**   Carbohydrate **16g**   Protein **15g**

This toothsome bread combines **warm spices** with dates and **ripe bananas** for a breakfast that's every bit **as good as dessert.**

Zucchini-Date
Breakfast Bread

 1 9×4-INCH (23×10CM) LOAF   15 MINUTES   55 MINUTES   ⅛ LOAF

INGREDIENTS

2 cups almond flour

2 TB. coconut flour

1 tsp. baking soda

¼ tsp. sea salt

1 TB. pumpkin pie spice

4 large Medjool dates, pitted and chopped

2 medium bananas, peeled

3 large eggs

1 tsp. apple cider vinegar

1 tsp. pure vanilla extract

¼ cup plus ½ tsp. melted coconut oil

1½ cups shredded zucchini

½ cup walnuts, chopped

¼ cup raw honey

METHOD

1 Preheat the oven to 325°F (170°C).

2 In a large bowl, combine almond flour, coconut flour, baking soda, sea salt, and pumpkin pie spice. Blend well with a fork until no clumps remain.

3 In a food processor, pulse Medjool dates, bananas, eggs, apple cider vinegar, vanilla extract, and ¼ cup melted coconut oil for 1 to 2 minutes, or until puréed.

4 Pour date mixture into dry ingredients, along with shredded zucchini and walnuts. Stir with a wooden spoon until completely combined.

5 Grease a 9×4-inch (23×10cm) loaf pan lightly with remaining ½ teaspoon melted coconut oil. Pour batter evenly into the pan. Bake for 45 to 55 minutes, or until a toothpick inserted into the center comes out clean.

6 Let bread cool before removing from the pan and slicing. Drizzle with raw honey to serve.

This bread makes an excellent base for Paleo French toast. Simply dip slices in beaten egg and fry in a lightly oiled pan, turning once, until egg has cooked through and is golden brown. Drizzle with grade-B maple syrup or raw honey, or top with fresh fruit, to serve.

EACH SERVING HAS:

Calories 385   Total Fat 28g   Carbohydrate 26g   Protein 11g

Tart and buttery lemon curd is a silky-smooth topping for crispy-edged, melt-in-your-mouth Paleo crêpes.

Paleo Crêpes with Lemon Curd

Lemon Curd

 1½ CUPS   2 HOURS, 10 MINUTES   15 MINUTES   2 TABLESPOONS

INGREDIENTS

3 large eggs

6 to 8 TB. raw honey

½ cup lemon juice

1 TB. lemon zest

¼ tsp. sea salt

6 TB. unsalted grass-fed butter, cut into cubes, or coconut oil

EACH SERVING HAS:

Calories **108**
Total Fat **7g**
Carbohydrate **11g**
Protein **2g**

METHOD

1 Working over a small bowl or ramekin, carefully separate 1 egg, allowing white to fall into the bowl and yolk to stay in one half of shell. Place separated yolk in a separate medium bowl. Repeat with another egg.

2 Discard both whites from 2 eggs or refrigerate for use in omelets or scrambles another time. Add remaining 1 egg (white and yolk) to yolks and whisk until fully incorporated. Set aside.

3 Place a small heavy-bottomed saucepan or double boiler over medium-low heat. A double boiler is best, or you can make one with a metal bowl that fits over a saucepan with about 2 inches (5cm) space between the bottom of the bowl and the bottom of the pan. Add 1 inch (2.5cm) water to the bottom pan before heating.

4 Add raw honey, lemon juice, lemon zest, and sea salt to the saucepan or top of the double boiler. Whisk constantly and heat just until warmed (about 85°F [30°C]).

5 Remove from heat. Carefully pour about ¼ cup of lemon mixture into eggs, and quickly whisk to avoid scrambling eggs. While whisking, pour in another ¼ cup of lemon mixture. Continue until lemon mixture is fully incorporated into eggs.

6 Using a rubber scraper, return mixture to the pan and place over medium heat. Gradually add cubes of unsalted grass-fed butter and stir constantly for 5 to 7 minutes, or until curd starts to thicken and tiny bubbles begin to surface. Remove from heat.

7 Strain curd through a mesh sieve or cheesecloth into small jars. Chill in the refrigerator for 2 hours (curd should get thick as it cools). Serve with Paleo Crêpes.

Paleo Crêpes

 2 LARGE CRÊPES   5 MINUTES   12 MINUTES   1 LARGE CRÊPE

INGREDIENTS

1 cup tapioca flour

1 cup full-fat coconut milk

1 large egg

¼ tsp. sea salt

½ tsp. coconut oil

METHOD

1 In a medium bowl, whisk tapioca flour, full-fat coconut milk, egg, and sea salt until fully incorporated. Set aside.

2 Heat a nonstick skillet or griddle over medium heat. Grease the skillet lightly with coconut oil.

3 When hot, pour ½ of batter onto the greased skillet and cook for 2 to 3 minutes, or until little bubbles start to form on the surface.

4 Turn over crêpe and cook for 2 to 3 minutes, or until lightly browned. Repeat with rest of batter. Serve with Lemon Curd.

EACH SERVING HAS:

Calories **445**   Total Fat **23g**   Carbohydrate **57g**   Protein **5g**

Aromatic cardamom and **clove** accent **rich almond flavors** in this citrus-heavy, warm breakfast cereal.

Spiced Almond and
Orange Porridge

 3 CUPS　　 **5 MINUTES**　　 **15 MINUTES**　　 **½ CUP**

INGREDIENTS

2 cups full-fat coconut or almond milk

Zest of 1 orange (about 1 TB.)

¼ tsp. ground cardamom or ground cinnamon

¼ tsp. ground cloves

¼ tsp. sea salt

1½ cups almond meal or flour

2 TB. whole or ground flaxseeds

2 large ripe bananas, peeled and smashed

2 TB. chia seeds

½ cup pecans, chopped

Grade-B pure maple syrup (optional)

METHOD

1 In a medium saucepan over medium heat, combine full-fat coconut milk, orange zest, cardamom, cloves, and sea salt. Cook for 3 to 5 minutes, stirring occasionally.

2 Add almond meal, flaxseeds, and smashed bananas. Continue to cook uncovered, stirring frequently with a wooden spoon, until bananas break down and porridge thickens slightly (about 6 to 8 minutes).

3 Stir in chia seeds and pecans, and drizzle with grade-B pure maple syrup (if using) to serve.

Traditionally, porridge like this might call for orange blossom water instead of orange zest. This fragrant Mediterranean ingredient can be found in many specialty markets.

EACH SERVING HAS:

Calories **471**　　Total Fat **38g**　　Carbohydrate **32g**　　Protein **10g**

These crumbly scones are filled with **chewy dried apricots** and **crunchy pistachios,** brightened with a hint of **lemon, honey,** and **warm nutmeg.**

Apricot and Pistachio Scones

 8 SCONES   **20 MINUTES**   **20 MINUTES**   **1 SCONE**

INGREDIENTS

3 cups almond flour

1 tsp. baking soda

½ tsp. freshly grated nutmeg

½ tsp. sea salt

¼ cup cold coconut oil or unsalted butter

2 large eggs

2 TB. raw honey

2 TB. lemon juice

1 cup dried apricots, chopped

½ cup pistachios, chopped

EACH SERVING HAS:

Calories **383**

Total Fat **29g**

Carbohydrate **22g**

Protein **11g**

METHOD

1 Preheat the oven to 350°F (180°C).

2 In a large bowl, mix almond flour, baking soda, nutmeg, and sea salt until fully combined.

3 Add cold coconut oil and, using two metal forks, cut in pieces of oil until a crumbly mixture forms.

4 In a medium bowl, whisk together eggs, raw honey, and lemon juice. Add wet mixture to dry mixture, and combine with a wooden spoon. Gently mix in apricots and pistachios.

5 Form dough into 8 small balls. Place each ball on a parchment-lined baking sheet and press to flatten slightly.

6 Bake scones for 18 to 20 minutes, or until a toothpick inserted into the center of a scone comes out clean. Serve warm out of the oven.

Alternately, this recipe can be baked in a 10-inch (25cm) cast-iron skillet. Reduce the oven temperature to 325°F (170°C), and bake for 30 to 35 minutes.

Silky smooth and **tangy, to boot,** this Paleo yogurt is bound to become a **staple** in your Mediterranean kitchen.

Coconut Yogurt with Fresh Fruit

 2 CUPS   **1 HOUR, 15 MINUTES**   **12 TO 24 HOURS**   **½ CUP**

INGREDIENTS

4 (14-fl.-oz.; 400ml) cans full-fat coconut milk

2 probiotic acidophilus bifida gel capsules

Fresh seasonal fruit of choice

METHOD

1 Refrigerate full-fat coconut milk for at least 1 hour. When chilled, coconut milk should settle to the bottom of the can, with creamy coconut fat on top.

2 Carefully remove fat (coconut cream) from the top of each can and place in a sterilized quart glass Mason jar. Also add ½ cup coconut milk from the bottom of each can. Discard remaining milk, or use for something else.

3 Break probiotic acidophilus bifida gel capsules and empty contents into the jar of coconut cream. Using a clean metal spoon, stir until probiotics and coconut cream are completely combined.

4 Place a sterilized lid and metal ring on the jar and close tightly.

5 Wrap the jar with a large towel and place in a cooler with a heating pad set on low for 12 to 24 hours. Alternately, place the jar in the oven with the door closed and the oven light on. Yogurt should stay between 105°F and 110°F (40°C and 43°C).

6 Yogurt will continue to get tangier the longer it sits. Chill before serving with fresh seasonal fruit.

EACH SERVING HAS:

Calories **169**
Total Fat **1g**
Carbohydrate **73g**
Protein **10g**

To sterilize a glass Mason jar, submerge the jar, a new lid, and a metal ring in water. Place over high heat and boil for 5 minutes. Carefully remove the sterilized jar, lid, and ring with tongs, and place on a clean towel. (Never place the hot jar on a cold surface, or it may break.)

antipasto

Sometimes you just need a little premeal snack. These recipes are designed as starters, hors d'oeuvres, or small-portion snacks. Many are also excellent as party appetizer platters. And because no Mediterranean meal is complete without bread, I've also included a few grain-free options, along with several regional spreads.

Easy, **chewy,** and **delicious,** these quick Paleo flatbreads are a satisfying way to include **grain-free breads** in your day.

Grain-Free **Flatbread**

 8 FLATBREADS   **5 MINUTES**   **7 MINUTES**   **2 FLATBREADS**

INGREDIENTS

½ cup almond flour

½ cup tapioca flour

¾ tsp. sea salt

½ cup canned full-fat coconut milk

2 TB. extra-virgin olive oil

METHOD

1 In a medium bowl, combine almond flour, tapioca flour, sea salt, and full-fat coconut milk.

2 Place a medium nonstick skillet over medium-low heat. When the skillet is hot, add extra-virgin olive oil and wait 30 seconds.

3 Drop ¼ cup batter in the skillet and use a wooden spoon to spread batter into a flat disk.

4 Cook for 3 to 4 minutes, or until golden brown. Turn over and cook for 2 to 3 minutes. Repeat with remaining batter.

5 Serve warm or at room temperature.

> This flatbread recipe is so versatile, it's bound to become a Paleo kitchen standby. Add fresh garlic and rosemary, or try cinnamon and cardamom for a spiced twist.

EACH SERVING HAS:

| Calories 237 | Total Fat 18g | Carbohydrate 18g | Protein 4g |

This **blazing-hot salsa** gets its intense flavor from **green serrano chiles, fresh garlic cloves,** and a **warm spice blend** of **cumin** and **cardamom.**

Green **Zhug**

 2 CUPS   **10 MINUTES**   **NONE**   **¼ CUP**

INGREDIENTS

2 bunches fresh cilantro (about 2 cups, chopped)

2 to 6 green serrano chiles

4 garlic cloves

3 TB. extra-virgin olive oil

Juice of ½ lemon (about 1 TB.)

1 tsp. ground cumin

¼ tsp. ground cardamom

½ tsp. freshly ground black pepper

1 tsp. sea salt

METHOD

1 Cut stems off cilantro bunches. (Don't worry about stems remaining near leaves; just be sure to cut off bases.) Discard stems.

2 Slice stem tops off serrano chiles and cut each in half. Remove seeds and white sections. Discard stems, seeds, and white membranes.

3 Place cilantro leaves, serrano chiles, garlic, extra-virgin olive oil, lemon juice, cumin, cardamom, black pepper, and sea salt in a food processor.

4 Blend on high for 30 seconds, or until a chunky, salsalike consistency is formed. Adjust salt, if needed.

5 Serve as a spread with Grain-Free Flatbread or crackers.

Variation: To make **Red Zhug,** simply use red serranos instead of green, and add ⅛ teaspoon ground cloves. Fully ripened red serranos are often hotter than the unripened green variety, so you may want to use a few less in this recipe.

Chile oils and fumes can burn, so it's a good idea to wear disposable or rubber kitchen gloves when handling them. Wash your hands thoroughly with soap and warm water afterward to get rid of any oils, and try not to touch your eyes or face right after handling.

EACH SERVING HAS:

Calories 54	Total Fat 5g	Carbohydrate 2g	Protein 0g

Smoky paprika, nutty roasted cauliflower, and sweet red peppers combine to make the perfect preparty Paleo snack.

Roasted Red Pepper **Hummus**

 4 CUPS   15 MINUTES   30 MINUTES   ½ CUP

INGREDIENTS

1 large cauliflower, cut into florets

5 garlic cloves

2 TB. extra-virgin olive oil

½ tsp. ground cumin

¾ cup roasted red bell peppers or piquillo peppers, chopped

½ cup tahini

Juice of 1 lemon (about 2 TB.)

½ tsp. sea salt

¼ tsp. smoked paprika

METHOD

1 Preheat the oven to 350°F (180°C).

2 On a large rimmed baking sheet, spread cauliflower florets and garlic. Drizzle with extra-virgin olive oil and sprinkle with cumin.

3 Bake for 25 to 30 minutes, or until cauliflower is tender, stirring with a wooden spoon every 10 to 15 minutes. Remove from the oven.

4 Scrape warm cauliflower and garlic into a food processor fitted with a chopping blade. Add red bell peppers, tahini, lemon juice, sea salt, and smoked paprika.

5 Process to a smooth consistency. Taste; adjust sea salt and lemon juice, if desired.

6 Serve warm or chilled with Paleo crackers or vegetable slices.

> You can find roasted red bell peppers in a jar in most grocery stores, and cans of tangy Spanish piquillo peppers can be found at many specialty markets. Note that many canned piquillo peppers have added sugar, so you may wish to leave them out for that reason.

EACH SERVING HAS:

| Calories | 132 | Total Fat | 10g | Carbohydrate | 9g | Protein | 5g |

Chewy, salty focaccia is topped with **kalamata olives, fresh rosemary,** and **crispy onion flakes.** This **grain-free** bread is just as delicious as the original!

Olive and Onion **Focaccia**

 1 9×9-INCH (23×23CM) LOAF   10 MINUTES   20 MINUTES   ⅛ LOAF

INGREDIENTS

1 cup tapioca flour

2 TB. coconut flour

2 tsp. sea salt

½ tsp. baking soda

3 large eggs

¼ cup canned full-fat coconut milk or cream

½ tsp. apple cider vinegar

6 TB. plus ½ tsp. extra-virgin olive oil

1 TB. onion flakes

1 tsp. fresh rosemary, chopped

¼ cup kalamata olives, pitted and halved

METHOD

1 Preheat the oven to 375°F (190°C).

2 In a medium bowl, combine tapioca flour, coconut flour, 1 teaspoon sea salt, and baking soda. Mix with a fork or sift to remove any clumps. Set aside.

3 In a stand mixer, beat eggs, full-fat coconut milk, apple cider vinegar, and 4 tablespoons extra-virgin olive oil. Add dry ingredients and beat until fully incorporated.

4 Lightly grease a 9-inch (23cm) square baking pan or 10-inch (25cm) cast-iron skillet with ½ teaspoon extra-virgin olive oil. Pour batter into the pan.

5 Sprinkle onion flakes and rosemary over batter, and place kalamata olives evenly on top.

6 Bake for 16 to 20 minutes, or until a toothpick inserted in middle of focaccia comes out clean.

7 Immediately brush remaining 2 tablespoons extra-virgin olive oil over bread, and sprinkle with remaining 1 teaspoon sea salt. Serve warm.

Variation: To make **Sun-Dried Tomato Basil Focaccia,** eliminate onion flakes, rosemary, and kalamata olives, and replace with ¼ cup chopped sun-dried tomatoes, 1 teaspoon granulated garlic, and 3 large fresh basil leaves, thinly sliced.

EACH SERVING HAS:

Calories **214**   Total Fat **16g**   Carbohydrate **16g**   Protein **3g**

Pungent **garlic** and **sweet, ripe tomatoes,** accentuated with nothing more than **olive oil** and **sea salt,** make this simple spread shine.

Fresh Tomato and Garlic
Spread

 3 CUPS   **10 MINUTES**   **15 MINUTES**   **¼ CUP**

INGREDIENTS

6 large tomatoes (about 2 lb.; 1kg)

4 garlic cloves, finely minced

2 TB. extra-virgin olive oil

½ tsp. sea salt

This spread is excellent as a topping for fish or chicken. It can also be used as a marinade for meat, cheese, or vegetables.

METHOD

1 Fill a 4- to 5-quart (4 to 5L) pot with 3 quarts (3L) water. Cover and place over high heat until water comes to a boil (large bubbles breaking on the surface).

2 Meanwhile, using a small paring knife, carefully score an "X" on the bottom of each tomato. Make sure to cut just through skin and not into flesh of tomato.

3 While waiting for water to boil, fill a large bowl with ice water and set it next to the stove, along with a slotted spoon or skimmer.

4 When water comes to a boil, carefully drop tomatoes into the pot (being careful hot water doesn't splash out). Cook for 45 to 60 seconds, or until skins wrinkle slightly.

5 Using the slotted spoon, remove cooked tomatoes from boiling water and plunge immediately into ice water.

6 When tomatoes have cooled, remove from ice water. Carefully peel skins off each tomato, starting with skin next to the "X." Discard skins. Cut each tomato in half.

7 Place peeled tomato halves into a food processor fitted with a chopping blade. Add garlic, extra-virgin olive oil, and sea salt, and process on high for 30 to 45 seconds, or until puréed. Adjust sea salt, if desired.

8 Serve alongside Paleo bread or crackers.

EACH SERVING HAS:

| Calories 35 | Total Fat 2g | Carbohydrate 3g | Protein 1g |

This pungent spread combines **briny olives** and **anchovy fillets** with the unmistakable **flavor of preserved lemon.**

Olive and Preserved Lemon
Tapenade

 2 CUPS   5 MINUTES   NONE   ¼ CUP

INGREDIENTS

1 preserved lemon, seeds removed but rind intact

2 cups green or black olives, pitted

2 to 3 anchovy fillets, chopped

¼ cup flat-leaf parsley, chopped

2 TB. extra-virgin olive oil

¼ tsp. freshly ground black pepper

¼ tsp. crushed red pepper flakes

¼ cup toasted almonds, coarsely chopped (optional)

METHOD

1 Cut preserved lemon into thin slices (you'll need about 2 tablespoons).

2 In a food processor, pulse preserved lemon slices, green olives, anchovy fillets, flat-leaf parsley, extra-virgin olive oil, black pepper, crushed red pepper flakes, and almonds (if using) until a coarse mixture forms, or about 15 to 30 seconds.

3 Serve at room temperature or chilled, with crackers or fresh vegetable slices.

> Preserved lemons are whole lemons that have been packed in salt—releasing their natural juices to make a preserving solution—and stored for a minimum of 3 weeks to fully preserve. They can be found at most high-end and specialty grocery stores.

EACH SERVING HAS:

Calories **153**   Total Fat **15g**   Carbohydrate **5g**   Protein **3g**

Crispy, nutty, and **delicious,** these Paleo crackers are sure to please even the pickiest eaters.

Nut and Seed Crackers

40 CRACKERS   **20 MINUTES**   **20 MINUTES**   **4 CRACKERS**

INGREDIENTS

1 cup raw whole almonds

1 cup raw whole hazelnuts

½ cup raw pumpkin seeds

½ cup raw sunflower seeds

¼ cup flaxseeds

2 TB. chia seeds

2 TB. toasted sesame seeds (white or black)

2 tsp. whole caraway seeds

2 large eggs, slightly beaten

2 TB. coconut flour, for forming crackers (optional)

½ tsp. sea salt

METHOD

1 Preheat the oven to 350°F (180°C).

2 In a food processor, pulse almonds, hazelnuts, pumpkin seeds, sunflower seeds, and flaxseeds for 30 seconds to 1 minute, or until a course meal forms. Remove from the processor and place in a medium bowl.

3 Add chia seeds, toasted sesame seeds, and caraway seeds, and mix with a wooden spoon until fully combined. Add eggs and continue to stir until mixture forms a slightly sticky dough.

4 Cut 2 pieces of parchment paper to fit the bottoms of 2 large baking sheets (or use silicone sheet liners).

5 Form dough into 1-inch (2.5cm) balls. Place balls at least 6 inches (15.25cm) apart on baking sheets.

6 Using a pint-size Mason jar or flat-bottomed glass, press balls into thin, disclike crackers. (It may be helpful to press the jar or glass into coconut flour between pressings to keep dough from sticking to the glass.)

7 Sprinkle each cracker with sea salt. Bake for 15 to 20 minutes, or until lightly browned and crispy around the edges. Remove from the oven and let rest for 10 minutes.

8 Using a spatula, carefully remove crackers from the sheets and let cool completely on a wire rack before storing in an airtight container. Repeat steps 4 through 8 with any remaining dough.

Variation: To make **Garlic Rosemary Crackers,** add 1 teaspoon granulated garlic and 2 tablespoons fresh rosemary, finely chopped, to dough.

EACH SERVING HAS:

| Calories 218 | Total Fat 18g | Carbohydrate 9g | Protein 8g |

Smoky grilled vegetables are slathered with an aromatic sauce of jalapeño, garlic, and cilantro.

Grilled Vegetables with Mojo Verde

 1 CUP   **10 MINUTES**   **5 MINUTES**   **2 TABLESPOONS**

INGREDIENTS

2 medium zucchini, trimmed

2 medium red bell peppers, seeded and quartered

2 medium yellow bell peppers, seeded and quartered

4 to 6 asparagus spears, trimmed

6 large cremini or white button mushrooms, halved

6 TB. extra-virgin olive oil

½ tsp. smoked paprika (optional)

1 jalapeño, seeded

3 garlic cloves, crushed

1 cup fresh cilantro, chopped

1 cup fresh flat-leaf parsley, chopped

½ tsp. sea salt

METHOD

1 Preheat the grill to high.

2 Cut each zucchini in half lengthwise. Cut each half lengthwise again to make long, spearlike quarters.

3 In a large shallow dish or mixing bowl, combine zucchini, red bell peppers, yellow bell peppers, asparagus, cremini mushrooms, 2 tablespoons extra-virgin olive oil, and smoked paprika (if using), and toss until vegetables are fully coated. Set aside.

4 In a food processor, combine remaining 4 tablespoons extra-virgin olive oil, jalapeño, garlic, cilantro, flat-leaf parsley, and sea salt. Pulse for about 1 minute, or until puréed. Add more extra-virgin olive oil or sea salt, if desired. Place in a small serving bowl and set aside.

5 Place vegetables on the grill. Use a grill pan, if desired, or simply place longer vegetables crosswise against the grates to make sure they don't fall through. Grill for 1 to 2 minutes. Turn over and cook for 1 to 2 more minutes.

6 Remove from the grill. Serve roasted vegetables warm or chilled alongside Mojo Verde.

EACH SERVING HAS:

| Calories 129 | Total Fat 11g | Carbohydrate 8g | Protein 3g |

Buttery salmon with **tart capers** and **herbaceous fresh dill** form **flaky little cakes** fancy enough for any special occasion, but easy enough for an everyday meal.

Salmon Cakes with Capers and Dill

 6 SMALL CAKES 10 MINUTES 5 MINUTES 1 CAKE

INGREDIENTS

¾ lb. (340g) skinless salmon fillets, bones removed

1 large egg

1 TB. coconut flour

½ tsp. sea salt

1 TB. capers

1 TB. fresh dill, finely chopped

2 TB. extra-virgin olive oil

METHOD

1 Cut salmon fillets into 4 slices each. In a food processor, pulse salmon fillets for 15 to 20 seconds, or until roughly chopped.

2 In a medium bowl, whisk egg, coconut flour, and sea salt. Add salmon, capers, and fresh dill, and stir with a wooden spoon until fully combined.

3 Heat a medium skillet over medium-high heat. When the skillet is hot, add extra-virgin olive oil and wait 30 seconds.

4 Carefully drop a spoonful of salmon mixture into the hot skillet; it should sizzle. Drop remaining batter into the skillet until you have 6 cakes, spacing each spoonful at least 2 inches (5cm) apart.

5 Cook for 1 to 2 minutes, or until golden brown. Turn over each cake and press down lightly. Cook for 1 to 2 minutes, or until cakes are cooked through and golden brown.

6 Remove cakes from the hot skillet and place on a few paper towels to absorb any extra oil. Serve immediately.

These cakes are excellent topped with garlicky alioli or creamy tzatziki.

EACH SERVING HAS:

Calories **170**

Total Fat **13g**

Carbohydrate **1g**

Protein **12g**

Tiny bay shrimp steal the show in this cocktail salad with **toasty red peppers,** a splash of lemon, and a medley of **verdant fresh herbs.**

Bay Shrimp Cocktail Salad

 2 CUPS   **10 MINUTES**   **NONE**   **½ CUP**

INGREDIENTS

2 TB. fresh flat-leaf parsley, chopped

2 TB. fresh mint, chopped

2 TB. fresh basil, chopped

2 tsp. extra-virgin olive oil

Juice of ½ lemon (about 1 TB.)

1 lb. (450g) cooked bay shrimp

¼ cup roasted red peppers, sliced into ⅛-in. (3mm) strips

¼ tsp. sea salt, or to taste

⅛ tsp. freshly ground black pepper

METHOD

1 In a medium bowl, combine flat-leaf parsley, mint, basil, extra-virgin olive oil, and lemon juice.

2 Add bay shrimp and roasted red peppers, and stir with a wooden spoon until combined.

3 Add sea salt and black pepper, stir, and taste. Add more sea salt, if desired. Serve or refrigerate immediately.

This salad will keep nicely in the refrigerator for up to 24 hours. Most seafood gets mushy and odorous if kept longer than that.

EACH SERVING HAS:

Calories **140**   Total Fat **4g**   Carbohydrate **2g**   Protein **24g**

Piquant **Spanish-style chorizo** and **candylike Medjool dates** pair perfectly in these snappy little treats, drizzled with **peppery Aleppo honey.**

Chorizo-Stuffed Dates
with Aleppo Honey

 16 DATES   **15 MINUTES**   **25 MINUTES**   **2 DATES**

INGREDIENTS

1½ oz. (42g) hard Spanish-style chorizo

16 large Medjool dates, pitted

8 thin slices bacon, cut in half

2 TB. raw honey

½ tsp. ground Aleppo pepper or sweet paprika

EACH SERVING HAS:

Calories **205**

Total Fat **4g**

Carbohydrate **41g**

Protein **5g**

METHOD

1 Preheat the oven to 375°F (190°C).

2 Cut a piece of parchment paper to line the bottom of a large rimmed baking sheet (or use a silicone sheet liner).

3 Cut Spanish-style chorizo into 16 pieces, each about 1× ¼ × ¼ inch (2.5×.5×.5cm).

4 Stuff each pitted Medjool date with 1 chorizo piece. Wrap ½ bacon slice around each date and secure with a toothpick. Place wrapped dates on the baking sheet.

5 Bake for 15 minutes. Remove the baking sheet from the oven and carefully turn over each date.

6 Return to the oven and bake for 8 to 10 minutes, or until bacon is cooked through and crisp on top.

7 Meanwhile, in a small bowl, combine raw honey and Aleppo pepper. Drizzle over dates to serve.

Variation: If you want to avoid pork products, you can easily make **Manchego and Marcona Almond–Stuffed Dates** by substituting pieces of hard Manchego cheese for chorizo and stuffing a whole Marcona almond with cheese inside of each date. Skip wrapping each date in bacon, and instead bake for 4 minutes on each side.

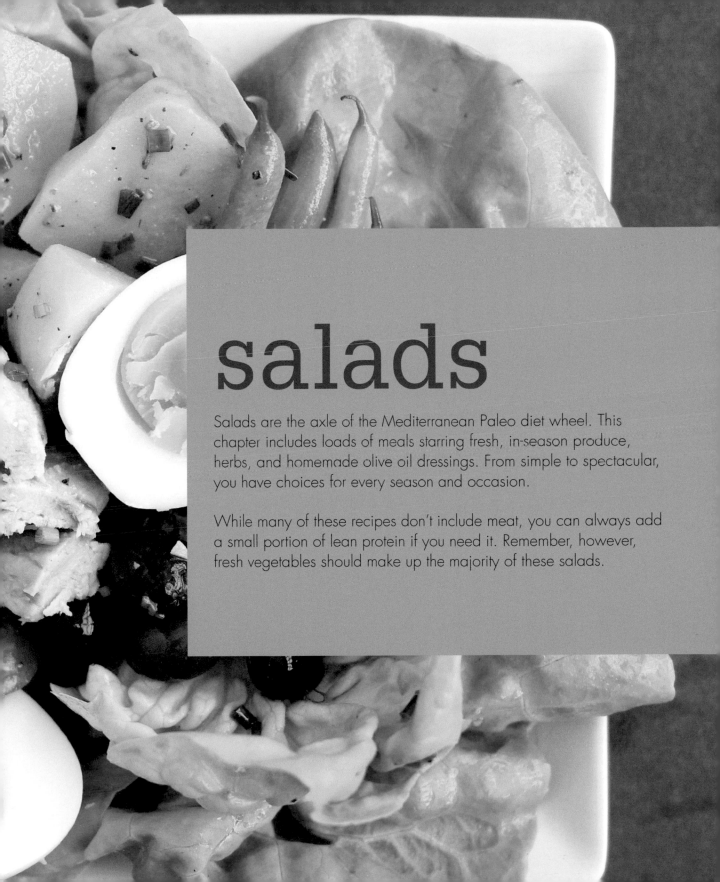

salads

Salads are the axle of the Mediterranean Paleo diet wheel. This chapter includes loads of meals starring fresh, in-season produce, herbs, and homemade olive oil dressings. From simple to spectacular, you have choices for every season and occasion.

While many of these recipes don't include meat, you can always add a small portion of lean protein if you need it. Remember, however, fresh vegetables should make up the majority of these salads.

Crunchy cauliflower, crisp celery, and **bell peppers** are combined with **sharp olives** and **toasty hazelnuts,** and then tossed together in a **creamy dill tzatziki.**

Cauliflower, Celery, and
Bell Pepper Salad with Tzatziki

CAULIFLOWER, CELERY, AND BELL PEPPER SALAD

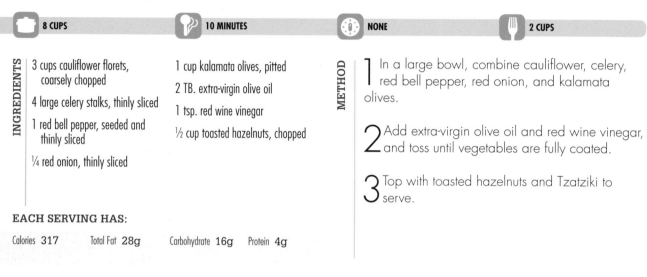

8 CUPS | 10 MINUTES | NONE | 2 CUPS

INGREDIENTS

3 cups cauliflower florets, coarsely chopped

4 large celery stalks, thinly sliced

1 red bell pepper, seeded and thinly sliced

¼ red onion, thinly sliced

1 cup kalamata olives, pitted

2 TB. extra-virgin olive oil

1 tsp. red wine vinegar

½ cup toasted hazelnuts, chopped

METHOD

1 In a large bowl, combine cauliflower, celery, red bell pepper, red onion, and kalamata olives.

2 Add extra-virgin olive oil and red wine vinegar, and toss until vegetables are fully coated.

3 Top with toasted hazelnuts and Tzatziki to serve.

EACH SERVING HAS:

Calories 317   Total Fat 28g   Carbohydrate 16g   Protein 4g

TZATZIKI

2 CUPS | 5 MINUTES | NONE | ¼ CUP

INGREDIENTS

15 oz. (420g) plain full-fat Greek yogurt (or use plain coconut milk yogurt)

1 TB. extra-virgin olive oil

Juice of ½ lemon (about 1 TB.)

¼ tsp. sea salt

¼ tsp. freshly ground black pepper

1 small cucumber, minced

2 TB. fresh basil, parsley, or dill, chopped

1 garlic clove, minced

METHOD

1 In a small bowl, whisk full-fat Greek yogurt, extra-virgin olive oil, lemon juice, sea salt, and black pepper until fully combined to make dressing.

2 Add cucumber, basil, and garlic, and stir until combined. Chill before serving with Cauliflower, Celery, and Bell Pepper Salad.

EACH SERVING HAS:

Calories 52   Total Fat 2g   Carbohydrate 4g   Protein 6g

In this salad, **juicy ripe watermelon** and **sweet red onion** are doused in a mixture of **refreshing herbs, olive oil,** and **tangy feta cheese.**

Fresh Watermelon Salad

 4 CUPS   **15 MINUTES**   **NONE**   **1 CUP**

INGREDIENTS

1 small (about 5 lb.; 2.25kg) seedless watermelon

20 large mint leaves (about ¼ cup), chopped

10 large basil leaves, chopped

¼ cup flat-leaf parsley, chopped

4 (1- to 2mm-thick) slices red onion, separated into rings

2 TB. extra-virgin olive oil

1 TB. pistachios, shelled and chopped

¼ tsp. coarse sea salt

¼ cup crumbled feta cheese (optional)

METHOD

1 Using a large chef's knife, carefully slice watermelon in half. Place flat side down and slice both halves into 1-inch-thick (2.5cm) slices.

2 Trim rind (including all green and white portions) and discard. Cut melon into 1×1-inch (2.5×2.5cm) cubes.

3 In a large salad bowl, combine watermelon cubes, mint leaves, basil leaves, flat-leaf parsley, and red onion.

4 Drizzle with extra-virgin olive oil and sprinkle with pistachios, coarse sea salt, and crumbled feta cheese (if using). Serve immediately.

> You can use whatever fresh herbs you have on hand for this recipe. Feel free to use cilantro, chives, dill weed, oregano, or a combination!

EACH SERVING HAS:

Calories **217**   Total Fat **13g**   Carbohydrate **18g**   Protein **6g**

Fattoush is a classic Lebanese salad of **toasted flatbread, crisp radishes, cucumber, mint,** and a **punchy lemon-garlic vinaigrette** with **tart sumac.**

Fattoush

 6 CUPS   10 MINUTES   20 MINUTES   3 CUPS

NGREDIENTS

1 or 2 Grain-Free Flatbreads or pitas

2 TB. extra-virgin olive oil

1 TB. fresh lemon juice

1 garlic clove, minced

3 TB. fresh mint, minced

2 tsp. sumac

¼ tsp. sea salt

2 medium radishes, trimmed and thinly sliced

1 medium tomato, diced

1 small cucumber, thinly sliced

2 green onions, sliced

1 head romaine lettuce, thinly sliced or shredded

METHOD

1 Preheat the oven to 350°F (180°C).

2 Cut Grain-Free Flatbreads into 1-inch (2.5cm) strips. Place strips on a metal baking sheet. Bake for 15 to 20 minutes, or until browned and crispy.

3 Meanwhile, in a small bowl, whisk extra-virgin olive oil, lemon juice, garlic, mint, sumac, and sea salt until fully combined to make dressing. Alternately, place ingredients into a small Mason jar, cover tightly with a lid, and shake vigorously until fully combined.

4 Break up toasted flatbread strips into smaller sections.

5 In a large bowl, toss toasted flatbread pieces, dressing, radishes, tomato, cucumber, green onions, and romaine lettuce until coated. Serve immediately.

> Sumac has a slightly tangy, bitter taste and adds a unique flavor that's hard to replicate. Ground sumac can be found in many specialty stores or online through a variety of suppliers.

EACH SERVING HAS:

Calories **484**   Total Fat **34g**   Carbohydrate **40g**   Protein **10g**

Jewels of **pomegranate** perch atop a bed of **peppery arugula** and **juicy tomatoes,** drizzled with a **sweet** and **pungent ras el hanout dressing.**

Pomegranate and
Fresh Herb Salad

 6 CUPS   **15 MINUTES**   **NONE**   **3 CUPS**

INGREDIENTS

1 ripe pomegranate

Juice of ½ lemon (about 1 TB.)

1 tsp. raw honey

2 TB. extra-virgin olive oil

1 tsp. ras el hanout

¼ tsp. sea salt (optional)

4 cups baby arugula

½ small shallot, thinly sliced or shaved

10 cherry tomatoes, quartered

½ cup fresh mint leaves, chopped

½ cup fresh cilantro, chopped

½ cup shelled and toasted pistachios

METHOD

1 Put on an apron to protect clothing. Fill a large bowl with water, leaving 2 inches (5cm) from top of water to the top of the bowl.

2 Using a sharp knife, carefully cut pomegranate in half and place both halves into water. Immediately wipe up any juice on the cutting board to prevent staining.

3 Keeping pomegranate fully submerged, carefully tear each half apart, separating red seeds from white pith and rind. Discard pith and rind.

4 Using a medium colander or mesh strainer, strain seeds from water. Discard water and return drained seeds to the bowl. Remove any remaining white pith. Set aside.

5 In a small bowl, whisk lemon juice, raw honey, extra-virgin olive oil, ras el hanout, and sea salt (if using) until fully combined to make dressing. Alternately, place ingredients into a small Mason jar, cover tightly with a lid, and shake vigorously until fully combined.

6 Add baby arugula, shallot, cherry tomatoes, mint, cilantro, and dressing to pomegranate seeds. Toss to coat. Top with toasted pistachios and serve immediately.

EACH SERVING HAS:

Calories **405**   Total Fat **29g**   Carbohydrate **34g**   Protein **10g**

Hemp seeds make the perfect Paleo base for this **Mediterranean salad**, tossed with **parsley, mint, tomato, cucumber,** and a hearty dose of **garlic** and **lemon.**

Hemp **Tabbouleh**

 6 CUPS 40 MINUTES NONE 1½ CUPS

INGREDIENTS

½ cup fresh flat-leaf parsley, chopped

½ cup fresh mint, chopped

2 garlic cloves, minced

4 medium tomatoes, diced

1 small Persian cucumber or ½ English cucumber, diced

1½ cups raw shelled hemp seeds

Juice of 1 lemon (about 2 TB.)

3 TB. extra-virgin olive oil

½ tsp. sea salt

METHOD

1 In a large bowl, combine flat-leaf parsley, mint, garlic, tomatoes, Persian cucumber, hemp seeds, lemon juice, extra-virgin olive oil, and sea salt.

2 Taste and add more lemon juice or sea salt, if desired. Chill for 30 minutes before serving.

Usually tabbouleh is made with bulgur wheat. Instead, this version calls for raw hemp seeds. Also called *hemp hearts,* these seeds are nutritional powerhouses loaded with protein, fiber, and omega-3 fatty acids.

EACH SERVING HAS:

Calories 513   Total Fat 43g   Carbohydrate 16g   Protein 23g

This quick pickle recipe uses **crisp English cucumbers, tangy balsamic vinegar,** and **fresh dill** to create a refreshing side salad.

Balsamic Cucumbers
with Dill

 2 CUPS   **15 MINUTES TO 12 HOURS**   **NONE**   **½ CUP**

INGREDIENTS

1 large English cucumber, ends trimmed

½ tsp. sea salt

2 TB. balsamic vinegar

2 tsp. extra-virgin olive oil

2 TB. fresh dill, chopped

METHOD

1 Carefully cut English cucumber into 1- to 2mm slices.

2 Place cucumber slices in a medium bowl. Add sea salt, balsamic vinegar, extra-virgin olive oil, and fresh dill, and stir to combine completely.

3 Let stand for 10 minutes, or cover and refrigerate for up to 12 hours. Stir again before serving.

Variation: This recipe is fantastic savory or sweet. To make **Balsamic Strawberries with Fresh Mint,** replace cucumber with 1 pound (450g) sliced strawberries, eliminate sea salt, and replace dill with fresh mint.

> You can use 2 to 3 small Persian cucumbers in this salad as well, or any small, tender pickling cucumber. If you can only find traditional cucumbers at the grocery store, you may want to peel off the tougher skins before slicing.

EACH SERVING HAS:

Calories **49**   Total Fat **2g**   Carbohydrate **7g**   Protein **1g**

Tender **pea shoots** and **sweet asparagus** star in this spring salad, adorned with crisp **radishes**, a bit of heat from a **Calabrian chile**, and **toasted hazelnuts**.

Pea Shoots with Asparagus and Radishes

 8 CUPS   15 MINUTES   NONE   4 CUPS

INGREDIENTS

2 TB. extra-virgin olive oil

Juice of ½ medium lemon (about 1 TB.)

¼ tsp. sea salt

⅛ tsp. freshly ground black pepper

4 cups fresh pea shoots (tender parts only)

8 medium asparagus spears, trimmed and sliced into 1-in. (2.5cm) pieces

6 medium radishes, trimmed and quartered

1 cup sugar snap peas, sliced in half

2 spring onions or scallions, thinly sliced

1 small Calabrian chile, diced, or ½ tsp. crushed red pepper flakes

½ cup toasted hazelnuts, coarsely chopped

METHOD

1 In a small bowl, whisk extra-virgin olive oil, lemon juice, sea salt, and black pepper until fully combined to make dressing. Alternately, place ingredients into a small Mason jar, cover tightly with a lid, and shake vigorously until fully combined.

2 In a large salad bowl, combine pea shoots, asparagus, radishes, sugar snap peas, spring onions, Calabrian chile, and dressing. Toss until vegetables are fully coated.

3 Top with toasted hazelnuts and serve immediately.

EACH SERVING HAS:

Calories 405

Total Fat 32g

Carbohydrate 25g

Protein 11g

This recipe is best saved for the spring season, when fresh pea shoots are tender and sweet. Use baby spinach as an excellent alternative any other time of the year.

This briny salad from Provence gets its flavor from **traditional niçoise olives, hearty tuna,** and a **zippy anchovy vinaigrette.**

Niçoise Salad

 4 CUPS   **10 MINUTES**   **20 MINUTES**   **2 CUPS**

INGREDIENTS

3 large eggs

6 small sunchokes or Jerusalem artichokes, peeled and halved

10 green beans or haricots verts, trimmed

2 TB. extra-virgin olive oil

1 tsp. white wine vinegar

1 tsp. Dijon mustard

¼ tsp. freshly ground black pepper

4 anchovies, minced

1 TB. fresh chives, chopped

1 head butter lettuce, chopped

8 cherry tomatoes, halved

½ cup niçoise olives, pitted

1 (5-oz.; 140g) can oil-packed albacore or yellowfin tuna, drained

METHOD

1 Place eggs in a small pot and cover with cold water. Place on high heat until water begins to simmer. Immediately remove the pot from heat, cover, and set a kitchen timer for 13 minutes.

2 When the timer sounds, carefully remove eggs and plunge in cold water until cooled. Remove eggs from shells and cut into quarters.

3 Meanwhile, place peeled sunchokes in a second medium pot, with 1 quart (1L) water. Place the pot on high heat, covered, until water begins to simmer.

4 Reduce heat to medium and continue to cook sunchokes for 4 to 6 minutes, or until slightly tender. Add green beans and cook for 30 more seconds. Strain vegetables and immediately submerge in cold water until cooled.

5 In a small bowl, whisk extra-virgin olive oil, white wine vinegar, Dijon mustard, and black pepper until fully combined to make dressing. Alternately, place ingredients into a small Mason jar, cover tightly with a lid, and shake vigorously until fully combined. Add anchovies and chives, and stir (or shake) again.

6 In a large salad bowl, combine butter lettuce, cooled sunchokes and green beans, cherry tomatoes, niçoise olives, and dressing.

7 Toss until vegetables are fully coated with dressing. Top with albacore tuna and hard-cooked egg quarters to serve.

EACH SERVING HAS:

Calories **564**   Total Fat **40g**   Carbohydrate **10g**   Protein **31g**

This salad uses **crisp romaine** with a traditional combination of **sharp red onion, cool cucumber, tangy feta,** and **lemon Dijon dressing.**

Classic Greek Salad

 8 CUPS   **15 MINUTES**   **NONE**   **4 CUPS**

INGREDIENTS

2 TB. extra-virgin olive oil

Juice of ½ lemon (about 1 TB.)

1 garlic clove, minced

½ tsp. Dijon mustard

¼ tsp. sea salt

¼ tsp. freshly ground black pepper

1 large head romaine lettuce, chopped

8 cherry tomatoes, halved

4 red onion slices, halved

1 small cucumber, diced

½ cup kalamata olives, pitted and halved

½ cup crumbled feta cheese (optional)

METHOD

1 In a small bowl, whisk extra-virgin olive oil, lemon juice, garlic, Dijon mustard, sea salt, and black pepper until fully combined to make dressing. Alternately, place ingredients into a small Mason jar, cover tightly with a lid, and shake vigorously until fully combined.

2 In a large bowl, toss romaine lettuce, cherry tomatoes, red onion slices, cucumber, and dressing until vegetables are fully coated.

3 Top with kalamata olives and crumbled feta cheese (if using) to serve.

If you want a bit more protein in this meal, you can easily grill and slice a few boneless, skinless chicken breasts to add on top.

EACH SERVING HAS:

Calories **413**   Total Fat **32g**   Carbohydrate **28g**   Protein **8g**

Luscious fresh figs steal the show in this easy salad, accented with the sweet flavor of **balsamic vinegar** and tossed with **peppery arugula** and **pecans**.

Fig and Arugula Salad

 4 CUPS   10 MINUTES   NONE   2 CUPS

INGREDIENTS

2 TB. extra-virgin olive oil

2 TB. balsamic vinegar

¼ tsp. sea salt

¼ tsp. freshly ground black pepper

4 cups arugula

4 fresh figs, quartered

⅓ cup pecans, chopped

2 TB. chèvre (optional)

METHOD

1 In a small bowl, whisk extra-virgin olive oil, balsamic vinegar, sea salt, and black pepper until fully combined to make dressing. Alternately, place ingredients into a small Mason jar, cover tightly with a lid, and shake vigorously until fully combined.

2 In a large bowl, combine arugula, figs, pecans, and dressing. Toss until arugula is completely coated with dressing.

3 Top with chèvre (if using) to serve.

Fresh figs are a seasonal delight. If you can't find any, you can use fresh peaches, apricots, pears, or even segmented blood oranges. Use whatever fresh fruit is in season for this versatile recipe.

EACH SERVING HAS:

Calories **435**   Total Fat **33g**   Carbohydrate **33g**   Protein **9g**

Ruby beets and crisp raw carrots are tossed in a sesame-packed dressing of tahini and za'atar.

Beet and Carrot Slaw
with Tahini and Za'atar

 4 CUPS   15 MINUTES TO 24 HOURS   NONE   2 CUPS

INGREDIENTS

2 medium beets, trimmed and peeled

3 medium carrots, trimmed

2 large beet leaves, woody stems removed

1 TB. extra-virgin olive oil

2 tsp. lemon juice

1 garlic clove, minced

1 TB. tahini (sesame seed paste)

½ tsp. za'atar

1 TB. toasted sesame seeds (white or black)

METHOD

1 Using the grater disk on a food processor, shred beets and carrots. (Alternately, use a hand grater to make medium shreds.) Using a sharp knife, thinly slice beet leaves.

2 In a small bowl, whisk extra-virgin olive oil, lemon juice, garlic, tahini, and za'atar until fully combined to make dressing. Alternately, place ingredients into a small Mason jar, cover tightly with a lid, and shake vigorously until fully combined.

3 In a large bowl, combine beets, carrots, beet leaves, and dressing. Toss until vegetables are fully coated with dressing. Top with sesame seeds.

4 Serve immediately, or let marinate for up to 24 hours in the refrigerator.

Variation: This salad is also excellent with 2 medium apples and 2 medium raw kohlrabi or jicama instead of beets and carrots to make **Apple and Kohlrabi Slaw with Tahini and Za'atar.**

EACH SERVING HAS:

Calories 272

Total Fat 14g

Carbohydrate 34g

Protein 6g

Za'atar is a traditional Middle Eastern and North African spice blend made of dried thyme, oregano, marjoram, toasted sesame seeds, salt, and often sumac. It can be found in many specialty grocery stores and spice stores, and online.

paleo
pastas

How can pasta be Paleo? With vegetable noodles! These dishes make it easy to add a few extra servings to your diet using root vegetables, zucchini, and even shaved asparagus. Simply use a vegetable spiralizer, julienne peeler, or julienne plate on a mandoline to create your noodles. Or, while a bit more time consuming, use a regular peeler to make flat vegetable ribbons to use like linguine. Raw or cooked, these pastas make vibrant vegetable-based meals.

Mellow **celery root** makes the perfect base for this pasta with **sweet fresh clams,** juicy **cherry tomatoes, golden toasted garlic,** and a spritz of **white wine.**

Celery Root Spaghetti
with Clams

 8 CUPS   **15 MINUTES**   **12 MINUTES**   **2 CUPS**

INGREDIENTS

Juice of 1 medium lemon (about 2 TB.)

2 large celery roots

2 TB. extra-virgin olive oil

2 garlic cloves, minced

20 cherry tomatoes (about 1 cup), halved

¼ tsp. crushed red pepper flakes

2 TB. dry white wine

2 lb. (1kg) small live hard-shell clams, shells rinsed

½ cup flat-leaf parsley

¼ tsp. sea salt

¼ tsp. freshly ground black pepper

METHOD

1 Fill a large bowl, deep enough to hold both celery roots, halfway with water. Add 1 tablespoon lemon juice.

2 Working on 1 celery root at a time, trim both root and stem ends. Using a paring knife or vegetable peeler, carefully peel off rough outer skin. Immediately submerge peeled root in lemon water. Repeat with second celery root.

3 Use a vegetable spiralizer to create thin spaghetti strands with each celery root. Return "noodles" to lemon water. Alternately, use a vegetable peeler to create thin ribbons or strips.

4 Place a large skillet over medium-high heat. When the skillet is hot, add extra-virgin olive oil and wait 30 seconds.

5 Add garlic, cherry tomatoes, and crushed red pepper flakes, and sauté, stirring constantly, for 2 to 3 minutes, or until garlic is golden brown and tomatoes have blistered.

6 Add dry white wine and continue to stir, scraping up any browned bits off the bottom of the skillet. Add hard-shell clams, cover, and cook for 5 minutes.

7 Uncover, stir, and add strained celery root noodles. Cover again and cook for 3 to 4 minutes, or until clams have opened.

8 Remove from heat. Stir in flat-leaf parsley, sea salt, black pepper, and remaining 1 tablespoon lemon juice. Discard any clams that didn't open, and serve immediately.

EACH SERVING HAS:

Calories **309**   Total Fat **9g**   Carbohydrate **27g**   Protein **18g**

Thinly shaved asparagus ribbons and **sweet peas** are served carbonara style: with **crisp pancetta nuggets** and a **decadently rich sauce.**

Shaved Asparagus
Carbonara

 4 CUPS **15 MINUTES** **10 MINUTES** **2 CUPS**

INGREDIENTS

1 lb. (450g) thick asparagus spears (about 20 spears), trimmed

¼ lb. (115g) thick sliced bacon or pancetta, diced

1 medium shallot, minced

2 TB. dry white wine

½ cup shelled peas or thawed previously frozen peas

1 large egg yolk

¼ tsp. freshly ground black pepper

METHOD

1 Using a mandoline or vegetable peeler, carefully slice asparagus spears lengthwise into long ribbons. Set aside.

2 Place a large skillet over medium-low heat. Add bacon and slowly brown, turning once or twice, until crisp (about 3 to 4 minutes). Remove from the skillet and place on a paper towel to absorb grease.

3 Reheat the skillet with any remaining bacon grease over medium-low heat.

4 Add shallot and cook, stirring frequently, for 1 to 2 minutes, or until slightly translucent.

5 Carefully add dry white wine (watching out for any grease splatters), and stir with a wooden spoon to loosen any browned bits from the bottom of the skillet.

6 Add peas and cook for 1 minute. Turn off heat and move the skillet off the burner. Add asparagus, cover, and steam lightly for 1 minute.

7 Add egg yolk to hot vegetables, and toss to combine and cook egg. Top with crisp bacon and black pepper to serve.

Variation: If you don't have a good way to shave asparagus, this recipe is just as tasty with zucchini or celery root noodles instead.

EACH SERVING HAS:

| Calories 376 | Total Fat 19g | Carbohydrate 16g | Protein 14g |

A pesto of mild **carrot tops** and **toasted hazelnuts** steals the show, paired with spiralized carrots, sun-dried tomatoes, artichoke hearts, and **sautéed chicken**.

Carrot Spirals with
Carrot Top Pesto

 6 CUPS   **15 MINUTES**   **5 MINUTES**   **1½ CUPS**

INGREDIENTS

1½ lb. (680g) carrots, with greens

1 cup fresh basil, chopped

2 garlic cloves

Juice of ½ medium lemon (about 1 TB.)

2 TB. pumpkin seeds

¼ cup toasted hazelnuts

½ cup plus 1 TB. extra-virgin olive oil

½ tsp. sea salt

½ lb. (225g) boneless, skinless chicken breast, diced

¼ cup sun-dried tomatoes, coarsely chopped

⅓ cup canned artichoke hearts, chopped

METHOD

1 Trim greens off carrots. Cut off long stems and discard. Roughly chop leaves.

2 In a food processor, pulse carrot top leaves (about 2 cups), basil, garlic, lemon juice, pumpkin seeds, toasted hazelnuts, ½ cup extra-virgin olive oil, and sea salt until a smooth paste forms. Set aside.

3 Use a vegetable spiralizer to create thin spaghetti strands with each carrot. Alternately, use a vegetable peeler to create thin ribbons or strips.

4 Place a large skillet over medium-high heat. When the skillet is hot, add remaining 1 tablespoon extra-virgin olive oil and wait 30 seconds.

5 Add diced chicken breast and sauté, stirring frequently, for 2 to 3 minutes, or until chicken is browned and cooked through.

6 Add sun-dried tomatoes, artichoke hearts, and carrot spirals, and cook for 1 to 2 minutes, or until heated through. Remove from heat.

7 Add several tablespoons pesto to the skillet and toss to fully coat. Serve immediately.

EACH SERVING HAS:

| Calories 545 | Total Fat 38g | Carbohydrate 35g | Protein 20g |

Plump shrimp are steamed with **earthy cremini mushrooms** and **capers,** and tossed with **fresh basil, oregano,** and **thick zucchini ribbon linguine.**

Shrimp and Basil
Linguine

 6 CUPS   **15 MINUTES**   **10 MINUTES**   **3 CUPS**

INGREDIENTS

2 medium zucchini, trimmed

¼ tsp. sea salt

2 tsp. extra-virgin olive oil

2 garlic cloves, minced

6 medium cremini mushrooms, sliced

2 tsp. capers, rinsed

2 TB. dry white wine

½ lb. (225g) raw shrimp, any size

¼ cup fresh basil, chopped

2 TB. fresh oregano, chopped

⅛ tsp. freshly ground black pepper

Juice of ½ medium lemon (about 1 TB.)

METHOD

1 Using a vegetable peeler, peel each zucchini lengthwise to create noodlelike ribbons. Sprinkle with ⅛ teaspoon sea salt, massage gently to spread out salt, and place zucchini in a strainer over the sink.

2 Place a large skillet over medium-high heat. When the skillet is hot, add extra-virgin olive oil and wait 30 seconds.

3 Add garlic, cremini mushrooms, and capers, and sauté, stirring frequently, for 3 to 5 minutes, or until garlic is golden brown and mushrooms are tender.

4 Add dry white wine and stir, scraping up any browned bits off the bottom of the skillet. Add shrimp and cover, cooking, for 2 to 5 minutes, or until bright pink.

5 Remove from heat. Stir in zucchini ribbons, basil, oregano, remaining ⅛ teaspoon sea salt, black pepper, and lemon juice. Serve immediately.

EACH SERVING HAS:

Calories **232**   Total Fat **7g**   Carbohydrate **16g**   Protein **23g**

Hearty spaghetti squash with **za'atar** is smothered in **roasted endive** and a briny, nutty tapenade.

Spaghetti Squash with
Endive and Walnut Tapenade

 8 CUPS 20 MINUTES 40 MINUTES 2 CUPS

INGREDIENTS

1 (3-lb.; 1.5kg) spaghetti squash

¾ cup walnuts

¾ cup kalamata olives

½ cup flat-leaf parsley

2 garlic cloves, minced

¼ cup plus 2 TB. extra-virgin olive oil

Juice of ½ medium lemon (about 1 TB.)

1 TB. za'atar

4 small heads endive, quartered lengthwise

METHOD

1 Preheat the oven to 350°F (180°C).

2 Slice spaghetti squash in half from stem to blossom end. Scoop out seeds with a sturdy spoon and discard.

3 Place spaghetti squash halves face down in an ovenproof baking dish with ½ inch (1.25cm) water. Bake for 35 to 40 minutes, or until rind is soft to the touch.

4 Meanwhile, place walnuts, kalamata olives, flat-leaf parsley, garlic, ¼ cup extra-virgin olive oil, and lemon juice in a food processor. Pulse for 15 to 30 seconds, or until a rough paste forms. Set aside.

5 In a medium bowl, combine remaining 2 tablespoons extra-virgin olive oil and za'atar with endive quarters. Toss to coat endive completely.

6 Spread endive on a rimmed metal baking sheet. Bake alongside spaghetti squash, stirring once, for 15 to 20 minutes, or until edges are crisped.

7 Remove spaghetti squash and endive from the oven. Using a metal fork, loosen and remove noodlelike strands from squash halves and discard empty rinds.

8 To serve, top spaghetti squash strands with roasted endive quarters and walnut tapenade.

EACH SERVING HAS:

Calories 643   Total Fat 57g   Carbohydrate 35g   Protein 6g

Rich, **sweet potato spirals** are tossed in a **spicy tomato sauce** and topped with **hearty chicken meatballs** brimming with **fresh vegetables** and **oregano.**

Sweet Potato Pasta with
Tomatoes and Meatballs

 4 CUPS PASTA AND 12 MEATBALLS **20 MINUTES** **50 MINUTES** **1 CUP PASTA AND 3 MEATBALLS**

INGREDIENTS

- 2 medium sweet potatoes, peeled
- 2 TB. extra-virgin olive oil
- 1 medium carrot, peeled and minced
- 4 cloves garlic, minced
- 1 (28-oz.; 800g) can diced tomatoes
- 1 TB. Italian seasoning
- ¼ tsp. crushed red pepper flakes (optional)
- 1½ tsp. sea salt
- ½ tsp. freshly ground black pepper
- 1 red bell pepper, seeded and coarsely chopped
- 4 medium white button mushrooms
- ¼ cup fresh oregano, chopped
- 1 lb. (450g) ground chicken

METHOD

1 Use a vegetable spiralizer to create thin spaghetti strands with each sweet potato. Alternately, use a vegetable peeler to create thin ribbons or strips. Set aside.

2 Place a medium Dutch oven or braiser over medium heat. When the Dutch oven is hot, add 1 tablespoon extra-virgin olive oil and wait 30 seconds.

3 Add carrot and sauté, stirring frequently, for 4 to 5 minutes, or until carrot pieces are slightly softened. Add 2 garlic cloves and continue to cook 1 to 2 minutes, or until garlic is golden brown.

4 Add diced tomatoes, Italian seasoning, crushed red pepper flakes (if using), ½ teaspoon sea salt, and black pepper, and stir to combine. Reduce heat to low, cover, and simmer, stirring occasionally, for 25 minutes.

5 Place red bell pepper, white button mushrooms, oregano, remaining 2 cloves garlic, and remaining 1 teaspoon sea salt in a food processor. Pulse for 15 to 30 seconds, until vegetables are roughly chopped.

6 Combine vegetables with ground chicken. Form into 12 meatballs.

7 When sauce is ready, stir in sweet potato noodles, cover, and steam for 10 minutes, or until noodles are slightly tender. Remove from heat.

8 Place a medium skillet over medium-high heat. When it's hot, add remaining 1 tablespoon extra-virgin olive oil and wait 30 seconds.

9 Fry meatballs in oil, turning to brown on all sides, for 7 to 10 minutes, or until cooked through.

10 Top pasta and sauce with meatballs to serve.

EACH SERVING HAS:

| Calories 377 | Total Fat 13g | Carbohydrate 31g | Protein 34g |

Tangy **piquillo peppers** and **spiced chorizo** are tossed with **fresh mussels** and served over al dente **fresh zucchini noodles.**

Zucchini Noodles with
Piquillo Peppers and Mussels

 4 CUPS 20 MINUTES 12 MINUTES 2 CUPS

INGREDIENTS

1 lb. (450g) live mussels, with beards removed

2 medium zucchini, trimmed

¼ tsp. sea salt

2 TB. extra-virgin olive oil

½ medium yellow onion, diced

1 oz. (25g) hard Spanish chorizo, diced

3 piquillo peppers or 1 roasted red bell pepper, thinly sliced

¼ cup dry white wine

¼ cup cilantro, chopped

METHOD

1 Soak live mussels in a bowl of cool water for 15 minutes. Rinse thoroughly.

2 Meanwhile, use a vegetable spiralizer to create thin spaghetti strands with each zucchini. Alternately, use a vegetable peeler to create thin ribbons or strips.

3 Place zucchini noodles in a colander in the sink. Sprinkle with sea salt and gently massage with clean hands to make sure salt fully covers noodles.

4 After mussels have been rinsed, place a large skillet over medium-high heat. When the skillet is hot, add extra-virgin olive oil and wait 30 seconds.

5 Add yellow onion and sauté, stirring frequently, for 3 to 5 minutes, or until onion is slightly translucent. Add Spanish chorizo and piquillo peppers, and cook, stirring occasionally, for 2 minutes.

6 Give zucchini noodles a squeeze to get rid of any extra moisture, and place in the skillet along with dry white wine and mussels.

7 Increase heat to high, cover, and cook for 4 to 5 minutes, or until mussels open.

8 Discard any unopened mussels. Stir, garnish with cilantro, and serve immediately.

EACH SERVING HAS:

Calories 442	Total Fat 23g	Carbohydrate 25g	Protein 34g

soups

Nothing beats a warm, satisfying cup of soup on a cold day—unless
it's a fresh, chilled bowl of gazpacho on a simmering summer
afternoon! Whatever the weather calls for, this chapter provides an
option. Cold, hot, broth-based, creamy purée, or hearty stew, these
recipes are simple and delicious.

Luscious ripe cantaloupe—brightened with **fresh lemon**, a hint of **ginger root**, and just a **touch of basil**—makes this chilled soup a summertime treat.

Chilled Cantaloupe and
Blood Orange Soup

 3 CUPS   **2 HOURS, 15 MINUTES**   **NONE**   **1 CUP**

INGREDIENTS

1 (3-lb.; 1.5kg) ripe cantaloupe

Juice of 1 medium blood orange (about 3 TB.)

2 tsp. freshly grated ginger root

Juice of 1 lemon (about 2 TB.)

2 TB. extra-virgin olive oil

½ tsp. sea salt

1 TB. fresh mint, finely chopped

METHOD

1 Cut cantaloupe. Remove seeds and rind, and slice into 1-inch (2.5cm) cubes.

2 Place cantaloupe, blood orange juice, ginger root, lemon juice, extra-virgin olive oil, and sea salt in a blender.

3 Pulse for 1 to 2 minutes, or until puréed. Chill for at least 2 hours.

4 Ladle soup into bowls and garnish with fresh mint to serve.

Variation: Use honeydew melon and fresh basil instead of cantaloupe and mint, and top with chopped macadamia nuts, to make **Chilled Honeydew and Basil Soup.**

Fresh ginger root is a natural anti-inflammatory, digestive aid, and immune booster. The sweet melon in this recipe tones it down, but you may wish to add more if you love the unbridled flavor.

EACH SERVING HAS:

| Calories 187 | Total Fat 10g | Carbohydrate 25g | Protein 2g |

This classic Spanish soup has **mellow toasted garlic, smoked paprika,** and a creamy poached egg.

Sopa de Ajo

 4 CUPS   **5 MINUTES**   **20 MINUTES**   **2 CUPS**

INGREDIENTS

2 TB. extra-virgin olive oil

10 garlic cloves, minced

2 tsp. Spanish paprika

4 cups chicken stock or broth

½ tsp. sea salt

2 large eggs

1 TB. fresh cilantro, chopped

METHOD

1 Heat a medium saucepan over medium heat. When the pan is hot, add extra-virgin olive oil and wait 30 seconds.

2 Add garlic and cook, stirring continuously, for about 60 seconds, or until garlic is golden brown.

3 Add Spanish paprika and stir for 15 seconds. Add chicken stock and sea salt. Stir once, and continue to cook until small bubbles come to the surface (about 10 minutes).

4 While soup is simmering, gently break each egg into a separate small bowl.

5 With soup still simmering, gently slide each egg into hot liquid, using a small spoon to ladle a bit of stock over each egg.

6 Cover the pan and cook until egg whites are solid, about 3 to 5 minutes.

7 Ladle soup into bowls and top with fresh cilantro to serve.

Variation: Pair this soup with Cauliflower Steaks with Ras el Hanout for a heartier meal. Or slice a boneless, skinless chicken thigh and simmer it in broth for 10 to 12 minutes, until cooked through, for some extra protein.

EACH SERVING HAS:

| Calories 236 | Total Fat 19g | Carbohydrate 8g | Protein 9g |

Light and fresh, this quintessential summer soup has **ripe tomatoes, cucumber, bell pepper, fresh lemon juice,** and a dash of **hot sauce.**

Gazpacho

🍲 6 CUPS	🔪 15 MINUTES	⏱ NONE	🍴 1½ CUPS

INGREDIENTS

2 lb. (1kg) ripe tomatoes, coarsely chopped

1 medium sweet yellow onion, coarsely chopped

1 large cucumber, peeled and chopped

1 red bell pepper, seeded and coarsely chopped

3 garlic cloves, crushed

⅓ cup extra-virgin olive oil

3 TB. sherry vinegar

1 tsp. hot sauce (optional)

1 tsp. sea salt

½ tsp. freshly ground black pepper

½ cup chilled tomato juice

6 small lemon wedges

¼ cup fresh oregano, finely diced

METHOD

1 In a large bowl, combine tomatoes, yellow onion, cucumber, red bell pepper, garlic, extra-virgin olive oil, sherry vinegar, hot sauce (if using), sea salt, black pepper, and tomato juice.

2 Use a blender to purée smaller batches until smooth.

3 Ladle soup into small bowls, spritz with juice from lemon wedges, and garnish with oregano to serve.

EACH SERVING HAS:

Calories 268
Total Fat 20g
Carbohydrate 25g
Protein 4g

Everyone seems to have an opinion on what makes the best gazpacho. Chunky, smooth, sweet, or spicy—it's easy to change up this recipe to suit your preferences. You can also add basil, mint, or cilantro instead of oregano, if that's what you like.

Subtle **celery root** and **creamy leeks** classically flavor this **simple soup,** seasoned with **white pepper** and topped with a sprinkle of **fresh chives.**

Leek and Celeriac Soup

 6 CUPS   **20 MINUTES**   **30 MINUTES**   **1½ CUPS**

INGREDIENTS

1 TB. extra-virgin olive oil

1 TB. unsalted butter (or use additional extra-virgin olive oil)

6 medium leeks, sliced (white and light green parts only)

2 large celery roots, trimmed, peeled, and diced

1 qt. (1L) vegetable broth

1 tsp. sea salt

½ tsp. white pepper

2 TB. fresh chives, chopped

METHOD

1 Place a 3-quart (3L) pot over medium heat. When the pot is hot, add extra-virgin olive oil and unsalted butter (if using), and wait 30 seconds.

2 Add leeks and cook, stirring frequently, for 2 to 3 minutes, or until softened.

3 Add celery roots, vegetable broth, sea salt, and white pepper. Cover and simmer for 20 to 25 minutes, or until celery root is tender.

4 Taste, and adjust sea salt and white pepper, if necessary. Ladle soup into bowls and garnish with fresh chives to serve.

Variation: If you prefer puréed soups, simply blend finished soup until smooth before garnishing with chives.

Always be sure to clean leeks thoroughly to get any extra dirt off. It may be helpful to slice the leeks lengthwise before running under cool water.

EACH SERVING HAS:

Calories 237   Total Fat 7g   Carbohydrate 40g   Protein 2g

Subtle fennel and **saffron** flavor this French stew, allowing the soft and delicious tastes of the **fresh seafood** to shine through.

Bouillabase

 8 CUPS   15 MINUTES   25 MINUTES   2 CUPS

INGREDIENTS

12 saffron threads

3 TB. extra-virgin olive oil

4 garlic cloves, crushed

2 medium leeks, thinly sliced (white and light green parts only)

1 lb. (450g) medium fennel bulbs, trimmed and sliced, with tough inner core removed

1 tsp. sea salt

28 oz. (800g) canned, diced tomatoes (with juice)

2 qt. (2L) fish or vegetable stock

3 fresh thyme sprigs

1 bay leaf

½ tsp. orange zest or dried orange peel

½ lb. (225g) live mussels, cleaned and de-bearded

1 lb. (450g) live small Manila or steamer clams

½ lb. (225g) halibut, cod, or another firm whitefish fillet

4 fresh scallops, halved

½ lb. (225g) 16- to 20-ct. (about 8 to 10) raw shrimp, deveined

2 tsp. fennel fronds, finely chopped

METHOD

1 Place saffron threads in a small dish and add 1 tablespoon warm water. Set aside.

2 Heat a medium Dutch oven or braiser over medium-high heat. When the Dutch oven is hot, add extra-virgin olive oil and wait 30 seconds.

3 Add garlic, leeks, fennel, and ¼ teaspoon sea salt, and sauté, stirring frequently, for 3 to 4 minutes, or until tender.

4 Add tomatoes with juice, fish stock, thyme, bay leaf, orange zest, saffron (with residual water), and remaining ¾ teaspoon sea salt. Stir with a wooden spoon to combine. Bring to a simmer and cook, uncovered, for 15 minutes.

5 Add mussels and Manila clams. Stir to make sure all shells are submerged. Cover and cook for 2 to 3 minutes, or until mussels and clams open.

6 Add halibut, scallops, and shrimp, and stir. Cook for 30 seconds, or until opaque. Discard any mussels or clams that didn't open, as well as bay leaf.

7 Ladle soup into bowls, garnish with fennel fronds, and serve immediately.

EACH SERVING HAS:

Calories **411**
Total Fat **12g**
Carbohydrate **32g**
Protein **34g**

Straight from Tuscany, this savory soup has a **rich broth** flavored with **pancetta** and **aromatic vegetables,** and topped with **salty Parmigiano-Reggiano cheese.**

Soup alla Canavese

 8 CUPS 10 MINUTES 45 MINUTES 2 CUPS

INGREDIENTS

2 oz. (55g) pancetta or bacon, diced

1 TB. unsalted butter (optional)

1 medium yellow onion, diced

2 garlic cloves, minced

2 medium carrots, diced

1 large celery stalk, diced

3 TB. tomato paste

1 tsp. dried sage

1 tsp. sea salt

½ tsp. freshly ground black pepper

4 cups cauliflower florets, cut into small pieces

6 leaves lacinato kale, woody stems removed

1 bay leaf

5 cups chicken stock

2 oz. (55g) Parmigiano-Reggiano cheese, grated (optional)

METHOD

1 Heat a large soup pot or Dutch oven over medium-high heat. When the pot is hot, add pancetta. Cook, stirring frequently, for 2 to 3 minutes, or until pancetta is golden and crisp.

2 Add unsalted butter (if using), yellow onion, and garlic. Sauté, stirring frequently, for 3 to 5 minutes, or until onion is translucent and garlic is aromatic.

3 Add carrots, celery, tomato paste, sage, sea salt, and black pepper. Stir, and cook for 2 minutes.

4 Add cauliflower, lacinato kale, bay leaf, and chicken stock, and stir. Reduce heat to medium-low, cover, and simmer for 30 to 35 minutes, or until vegetables are tender. Remove and discard bay leaf.

5 Ladle soup into bowls and top with grated Parmigiano-Reggiano cheese (if using) to serve.

EACH SERVING HAS:

| Calories 262 | Total Fat 12g | Carbohydrate 27g | Protein 13g |

Nutty, roasted cauliflower is puréed into a **creamy soup** and drizzled with garlic and saffron–infused olive oil.

Puréed Cauliflower Soup
with Garlic and Saffron

 8 CUPS   10 MINUTES   30 MINUTES   2 CUPS

INGREDIENTS

1 large head cauliflower, cut into florets

1 large yellow onion, diced

3 TB. extra-virgin olive oil

½ tsp. sea salt

½ tsp. freshly ground black pepper

6 cups chicken stock

4 garlic cloves, sliced

8 to 12 saffron threads

METHOD

1 Preheat the oven to 375°F (190°C).

2 Spread cauliflower florets and yellow onion on a large rimmed baking sheet. Drizzle with 1 tablespoon extra-virgin olive oil, and sprinkle with sea salt and black pepper.

3 Bake cauliflower and onion for 15 to 25 minutes, or until golden brown. Meanwhile, in a large pan or soup pot over medium heat, warm chicken stock.

4 When done roasting, transfer cauliflower and onions to stock. Using an immersion blender, purée soup in the pan, or use a blender to purée smaller batches. Season with additional sea salt, if needed.

5 Shortly before serving, in a small skillet over medium-high heat, heat remaining 2 tablespoons extra-virgin olive oil.

6 When oil is hot, add garlic and sauté, stirring constantly, for 30 to 45 seconds, or until golden and crisped. Remove from heat immediately and stir saffron threads into garlic oil.

7 Ladle soup into bowls. Drizzle garlic and saffron oil over puréed soup to serve.

EACH SERVING HAS:

Calories 292   Total Fat 15g   Carbohydrate 28g   Protein 14g

This **creamy, sweet carrot soup** with **fragrant Moroccan spices** is garnished with **tangy yogurt, crunchy raw pumpkin seeds,** and **fresh cilantro.**

Moroccan Carrot Soup

 6 CUPS   **15 MINUTES**   **30 MINUTES**   **1½ CUPS**

INGREDIENTS

2 TB. extra-virgin olive oil

1 medium yellow onion, diced

2 garlic cloves, sliced

½ tsp. fresh ginger root, grated

2 tsp. Moroccan spice blend (see sidebar)

1 lb. (450g) carrots, peeled and diced

3 cups vegetable or chicken stock

½ tsp. sea salt

1 tsp. raw honey

1 tsp. fresh lemon juice

¼ cup full-fat coconut yogurt

2 TB. raw shelled pumpkin seeds

3 TB. fresh cilantro leaves

METHOD

1 Place a heavy-bottom soup pot or Dutch oven over medium-high heat. When the pot is hot, add extra-virgin olive oil and wait 30 seconds.

2 Add yellow onion and garlic, and sauté, stirring frequently, for 3 to 5 minutes, or until onion is slightly translucent.

3 Add ginger root and Moroccan spice blend, and cook, stirring occasionally, for 60 seconds, or until fragrant.

4 Add carrots, vegetable stock, and sea salt. Cover, reduce heat to medium, and simmer for 15 to 20 minutes, or until carrots are tender.

5 Remove from heat and add honey and lemon juice. Purée hot soup in smaller batches in a blender, or use an immersion blender in the pot, until smooth.

6 Ladle soup into bowls and garnish with full-fat coconut yogurt, pumpkin seeds, and fresh cilantro to serve.

To make Moroccan spice blend, simply combine ½ teaspoon each ground cumin, cinnamon, coriander, cayenne pepper, ground black pepper, allspice, and cloves.

EACH SERVING HAS:

| Calories 269 | Total Fat 8g | Carbohydrate 49g | Protein 8g |

vegetables

While vegetables star in so many recipes throughout this book, this chapter focuses on seasonal sides and mains. Often, with little more than good olive oil and a bit of sea salt, the naturally delicious flavors of fresh, seasonal produce shine.

Local farmer's markets are a valuable resource for sourcing exceptional vegetables, as you'll only be able to purchase what's currently in season. Soon you'll learn what time of year to expect certain vegetables and how to plan your menu accordingly.

Sweet roasted carrots are drizzled with lemon juice, honey, and crisp cumin seeds and served with a tangy side of full-fat yogurt.

Roasted Carrots with
Cumin and Yogurt

 20 CARROTS   **10 MINUTES**   **30 MINUTES**   **5 CARROTS**

INGREDIENTS

1 lb. (450g) small carrots, trimmed and halved lengthwise

2 TB. extra-virgin olive oil

1 tsp. raw honey

½ tsp. sea salt

½ tsp. freshly ground black pepper

1 tsp. whole cumin seeds

½ medium lemon, cut into 4 wedges

¼ cup full-fat yogurt or full-fat coconut cream (optional)

METHOD

1 Preheat the oven to 425°F (220°C).

2 In a medium bowl, toss carrots in extra-virgin olive oil and raw honey.

3 Spread carrots evenly over a metal baking sheet. Sprinkle with sea salt, black pepper, and cumin seeds.

4 Bake for 25 to 30 minutes, or until tender.

5 Squeeze fresh lemon juice over top and serve alongside full-fat yogurt for dipping.

This simple side is an absolute showstopper when you use purple, orange, yellow, and red carrots. These gorgeous rainbow carrots can often be found year-round at most high-end markets.

EACH SERVING HAS:

Calories **109**   Total Fat **7g**   Carbohydrate **11g**   Protein **1g**

Geometric Romanesco florets, paired with **pine nut crumbles,** are pan-seared until **golden brown** and served with **velvety saffron alioli.**

Romanesco with Pine Nuts and Saffron Alioli

ROMANESCO WITH PINE NUTS

 2 CUPS 10 MINUTES 6 MINUTES ½ CUP

INGREDIENTS

2 TB. extra-virgin olive oil

1½ lb. (680g) Romanesco, cut into small florets

2 TB. toasted pine nuts, finely minced or ground

¼ tsp. coarse sea salt

1 TB. fresh lemon juice

METHOD

1 Place a large cast-iron skillet over medium-high heat. When the skillet is hot, add extra-virgin olive oil and wait 30 seconds.

2 Add Romanesco and sauté, not stirring, for 2 to 3 minutes, or until deep golden brown on one side. Stir carefully and turn heat down to low.

3 Sprinkle toasted pine nuts, sea salt, and lemon juice on top. Cover and steam for 2 to 3 minutes, or until Romanesco is tender.

4 Let cool slightly before serving with Saffron Alioli.

EACH SERVING HAS:

Calories **150**   Total Fat **10g**   Carbohydrate **14g**   Protein **1g**

SAFFRON ALIOLI

 ¾ CUP   15 MINUTES   NONE   1 TABLESPOON

INGREDIENTS

6 to 8 saffron threads

1 tsp. warm water

1 large garlic clove, pressed or very finely minced

¼ tsp. sea salt

¼ tsp. Dijon mustard

1 large egg yolk, at room temperature

¾ cup extra-virgin olive oil, at room temperature

1 TB. fresh lemon juice

METHOD

1 Place saffron threads in 1 teaspoon warm water and let sit for 5 minutes.

2 Using the broad side of a knife, scrape garlic clove with sea salt until a fine paste forms. Alternately, use a mortar and pestle or a press to mash garlic into a smooth paste with no remaining chunks.

3 Place garlic paste, Dijon mustard, saffron threads (with residual water), and egg yolk into a wide-mouth pint-size Mason jar. Using an immersion blender, pulse mixture for 15 seconds, or until fully blended.

4 Add 2 drops extra-virgin olive oil and blend for 10 seconds. Add 2 more drops extra-virgin olive oil and blend for 10 seconds.

5 Continue adding oil 1 teaspoon at a time and blending at 10-second intervals until a mayonnaise consistency begins to form. At that point, pour in remaining extra-virgin olive oil and blend until fully incorporated.

6 Add lemon juice and blend until combined. Taste and adjust salt or lemon as needed. Serve with Romanesco with Pine Nuts.

Romanesco is a gorgeous brassica, closely related to both broccoli and cauliflower. It's quite distinct, due to the geometric pattern that looks like a fractal. While its texture is similar to cauliflower, the taste is slightly nuttier than its traditional counterpart.

EACH SERVING HAS:

Calories **126**   Total Fat **14g**   Carbohydrate **0g**   Protein **0g**

Bright radicchio is roasted to mellow the bitterness, slathered in **North African chermoula,** and topped with **crunchy toasted walnuts.**

Roasted Radicchio with
Chermoula and Walnuts

 12 QUARTERS   15 MINUTES   20 MINUTES   2 QUARTERS

INGREDIENTS

1½ cups cilantro

½ cup flat-leaf parsley

6 garlic cloves, sliced

1 tsp. ground cumin

1 tsp. smoked paprika

¾ tsp. sea salt

¼ tsp. cayenne pepper

½ cup extra-virgin olive oil

2 TB. fresh lemon juice

3 heads radicchio, quartered

½ cup walnuts, chopped

METHOD

1 Preheat the oven to 400°F (200°C).

2 To make chermoula, combine cilantro, flat-leaf parsley, garlic, cumin, smoked paprika, sea salt, cayenne pepper, extra-virgin olive oil, and lemon juice in a food processor. Pulse for 30 seconds, or until a paste forms. Taste and adjust seasonings, if desired.

3 Toss radicchio quarters in just enough chermoula to coat. Spread radicchio on a rimmed baking sheet. Bake for 12 to 15 minutes, turning once, until wilted and tender.

4 Meanwhile, place walnuts in a small skillet over low heat. Toast, stirring frequently, for 3 to 4 minutes, or until aromatic. Remove from the skillet immediately.

5 To serve, top roasted radicchio with toasted walnuts.

Chermoula is traditionally used as a topping for fish or seafood, but is just as tasty on vegetables, chicken, or lamb.

EACH SERVING HAS:

Calories **247**   Total Fat **25g**   Carbohydrate **6g**   Protein **3g**

This **zesty dish** of **roast celery root** with **fiery cayenne pepper** and **smoked paprika** is served with a **creamy garlic alioli** to tame the sting.

Celery Root "Patatas"
Bravas with Alioli

CELERY ROOT "PATATAS" BRAVAS

 6 CUPS **10 MINUTES** **30 MINUTES** **1 CUP**

INGREDIENTS

3 large celery roots, trimmed and peeled

3 TB. extra-virgin olive oil

1 tsp. sea salt

2 tsp. smoked paprika

1 tsp. cayenne pepper (use less or more as preferred)

METHOD

1 Preheat the oven to 350°F (180°C).

2 Chop celery roots into 1-inch (2.5cm) cubes. Toss cubes with extra-virgin olive oil, sea salt, smoked paprika, and cayenne pepper.

3 Cut a piece of parchment paper to line the bottom of a large rimmed baking sheet (or use a silicone sheet liner). Spread seasoned celery roots evenly over the baking sheet.

4 Bake for 20 to 30 minutes, stirring every 10 minutes, until firm but tender when pierced with a fork. Serve warm with a side of Alioli.

EACH SERVING HAS:

Calories **150**   Total Fat **7g**   Carbohydrate **19g**   Protein **0g**

ALIOLI

 ¾ CUP **10 MINUTES** **NONE** **2 TABLESPOONS**

INGREDIENTS

1 large garlic clove, pressed or very finely minced

¼ tsp. sea salt

¼ tsp. Dijon mustard

1 large egg yolk, at room temperature

¾ cup extra-virgin olive oil, at room temperature

1 TB. fresh lemon juice

METHOD

1 Using the broad side of a knife, scrape garlic clove with sea salt until a fine paste forms. Alternately, use a mortar and pestle or a press to mash garlic into a smooth paste.

2 Place garlic paste, Dijon mustard, and egg yolk into a wide-mouth pint-size Mason jar. Using an immersion blender, pulse mixture for 15 seconds, or until fully blended.

3 Add 2 drops extra-virgin olive oil and blend for 10 seconds. Add 2 more drops extra-virgin olive oil and blend for 10 seconds.

4 Continue adding oil 1 teaspoon at a time and blending at 10-second intervals until a mayonnaise consistency begins to form. At that point, pour in remaining extra-virgin olive oil and blend until fully incorporated.

5 Add lemon juice and blend until combined. Taste and adjust salt or lemon juice as needed before serving with Celery Root "Patatas."

EACH SERVING HAS:

Calories **192**   Total Fat **22g**   Carbohydrate **1g**   Protein **1g**

Crunchy Brussels sprouts and **mild flat-leaf parsley** are brightened with a squeeze of **fresh lemon juice** and topped with **toasty hazelnuts.**

Shaved Brussels with
Lemon and Parsley

 4 CUPS　　 **10 MINUTES**　　 **5 MINUTES**　　 **1 CUP**

INGREDIENTS

2 lb. (1kg) fresh Brussels sprouts, trimmed

1 TB. extra-virgin olive oil

¼ cup fresh flat-leaf parsley, chopped

Juice of 1 lemon (about 2 TB.)

¼ tsp. sea salt

¼ tsp. freshly ground black pepper

½ cup toasted hazelnuts, chopped

METHOD

1 Shred Brussels sprouts using a mandoline or the grater plate of a food processor, or by slicing thinly with a knife.

2 Place a large skillet over medium heat. When the skillet is hot, add extra-virgin olive oil and wait 30 seconds.

3 Add Brussels sprouts and sauté, stirring frequently, for 1 to 2 minutes, or until sprouts are vivid green but still crisp.

4 Stir in flat-leaf parsley, lemon juice, sea salt, and black pepper. Remove from heat.

5 Top with toasted hazelnuts to serve.

Variation: To make **Shaved Brussels and Apple with Basil,** substitute fresh basil for flat-leaf parsley, and grate a fresh apple to add in to Brussels sprouts just before serving for a hint of sweetness.

This recipe proves that Brussels sprouts don't have to be fully cooked to be enjoyable. Raw Brussels sprouts are an excellent salad or slaw base, and add a bit of color variety and a lot of fresh crunch to any vegetable mix.

EACH SERVING HAS:

Calories **222**　　Total Fat **13g**　　Carbohydrate **24g**　　Protein **10g**

Rich and robust Lebanese **seven-spice** blend seasons **earthy mushrooms** and **tomatoes,** which are baked inside vibrant purple eggplant.

Stuffed Eggplant with Lebanese Seven-Spice Blend

 4 EGGPLANT HALVES   **15 MINUTES**   **1 HOUR**   **½ EGGPLANT**

INGREDIENTS

2 medium eggplants, about 8 in. (20cm) long

2 TB. plus 1 tsp. extra-virgin olive oil

1 tsp. sea salt

½ tsp. freshly ground black pepper

1 medium yellow onion, diced

4 garlic cloves, minced

1 lb. (450g) medium cremini mushrooms, diced

2 medium tomatoes, diced

1 TB. Lebanese seven-spice blend

¼ cup flat-leaf parsley, chopped

¼ cup cilantro, chopped

2 TB. pine nuts, chopped

METHOD

1 Preheat the oven to 425°F (220°C).

2 Cut eggplants in half lengthwise. Using a spoon, scoop out and discard seeds and flesh, leaving a ½-inch (1.25cm) rim of eggplant.

3 Brush inside of each half lightly with 1 teaspoon extra-virgin olive oil. Sprinkle with ½ teaspoon sea salt and black pepper.

4 Place halves face up in a shallow baking dish. Bake for 15 to 20 minutes, or until lightly golden brown.

5 Meanwhile, place a medium skillet over medium-high heat. When it's hot, add 2 tablespoons extra-virgin olive oil and wait 30 seconds.

6 Add yellow onion, garlic, and mushrooms, and sauté, stirring, for 4 to 6 minutes, or until onion is translucent and mushrooms are soft.

7 Reduce heat to medium-low. Add tomatoes, Lebanese seven-spice blend, and remaining ½ teaspoon sea salt, and cook for 5 minutes, stirring frequently. Remove from heat. Stir in flat-leaf parsley and cilantro.

8 Remove golden eggplant halves from the oven. Reduce the oven temperature to 350°F (180°C).

9 Spoon vegetable mixture evenly into hollowed-out eggplant halves. Sprinkle with pine nuts.

10 Line the baking dish with aluminum foil and place eggplant halves on top. Bake for 15 to 20 minutes, or until halves are tender. Let cool slightly before serving.

EACH SERVING HAS:

Calories **222**   Total Fat **12g**   Carbohydrate **28g**   Protein **5g**

These sometimes **spicy**, sometimes **mild seasonal peppers** are **pan roasted** to perfection and tossed in nothing more than **good olive oil** and **coarse sea salt**.

Roasted Padróns
with Sea Salt

🥘 **2½ CUPS**　　🖐 **5 MINUTES**　　🕐 **10 MINUTES**　　🍴 **½ CUP**

INGREDIENTS

1 lb. (450g) whole Padrón peppers

1 TB. high-quality extra-virgin olive oil

½ tsp. coarse sea salt

METHOD

1 Place a medium cast-iron skillet over medium-high heat.

2 When the skillet is hot, place as many whole Padrón peppers on the bottom of the skillet as will fit. Keep a large bowl nearby, as well as a pair of tongs.

3 Cook peppers for 4 to 6 minutes, or until skins begin to blister and brown. Carefully flip peppers as needed to cook all sides evenly. Remove peppers to the bowl when uniformly browned and blistered. Repeat with any remaining peppers.

4 When all peppers have been cooked, add high-quality extra-virgin olive oil and sea salt, and toss to combine.

5 Serve whole peppers immediately with a small bowl on the side to collect discarded stems.

Make sure to keep the pepper stems intact. They make excellent handles for holding the warm peppers.

EACH SERVING HAS:

Calories **94**　　Total Fat **4g**　　Carbohydrate **2g**　　Protein **1g**

Roasted fennel, caramelized in **fresh orange juice**, is topped with **licorice-like tarragon** and **pecans** coated with just the right amount of **sweet** and **spice**.

Fennel with Tarragon
and Spiced Pecans

FENNEL WITH TARRAGON

 2 CUPS   **5 MINUTES**   **20 MINUTES**   **½ CUP**

INGREDIENTS

4 small fennel bulbs (or 2 large bulbs)

1 TB. extra-virgin olive oil

¼ tsp. sea salt

2 tsp. fresh tarragon, chopped

2 TB. fresh orange juice

EACH SERVING HAS:

Calories **107**
Total Fat **4g**
Carbohydrate **18g**
Protein **3g**

METHOD

1 Trim fronds and thinner stalks off each fennel bulb. Also trim each stem end. Cut halves into ¼-inch (.5cm) slices, removing tough inner core as you slice.

2 In a medium bowl, combine extra-virgin olive oil, sea salt, and tarragon. Add fennel and toss to coat completely.

3 Place a large cast-iron skillet over medium heat. When the skillet is hot, add fennel mixture and sauté, stirring frequently, for 15 to 20 minutes, or until golden brown and caramelized.

4 Add orange juice to the hot skillet and stir, scraping any browned bits off the bottom of the skillet.

5 Serve warm and top with Spiced Pecans.

SPICED PECANS

 2 CUPS   **5 MINUTES**   **20 MINUTES**   **¼ CUP**

INGREDIENTS

2 TB. coconut sugar

½ tsp. sea salt

½ tsp. cayenne pepper

¼ tsp. allspice

½ tsp. cinnamon

2 cups raw pecan halves

1 egg white, slightly beaten

EACH SERVING HAS:

Calories **226**
Total Fat **21g**
Carbohydrate **8g**
Protein **4g**

METHOD

1 Preheat the oven to 300°F (150°C).

2 Cut a piece of parchment paper to line the bottom of a large rimmed baking sheet (or use a silicone sheet liner).

3 In a medium bowl, combine coconut sugar, sea salt, cayenne pepper, allspice, and cinnamon.

4 In a separate bowl, toss pecans in egg white to coat completely. Using a slotted spoon or fork, remove pecans and toss in seasoning mixture.

5 Spread coated pecans on the baking sheet. Bake for about 20 minutes, stirring occasionally, until crisp. Serve by sprinkling on Fennel with Tarragon.

Thick, meaty slices of **cauliflower** are **blackened** in a **rich 12-spice blend** with a punch of piquant **cayenne.**

Cauliflower Steaks with
Ras El Hanout

 2 STEAKS   **5 MINUTES**   **6 MINUTES**   **1 STEAK**

INGREDIENTS

1 large head cauliflower

3 tsp. extra-virgin olive oil

2 TB. ras el hanout

¼ tsp. cayenne pepper

½ tsp. sea salt

METHOD

1 Using a large chef's knife, carefully cut cauliflower head through stem into 1¼-inch (3cm) slices. You may wish to cut it in half first, to make it easier to slice.

2 In a small bowl, combine 1 teaspoon extra-virgin olive oil, ras el hanout, cayenne pepper, and sea salt. Rub mixture on all sides of cauliflower steaks.

3 Place a large skillet over medium-high heat. When the skillet is hot, add remaining 2 teaspoons extra-virgin olive oil and wait 30 seconds.

4 Place cauliflower steaks in hot oil. Fry without moving for 2 to 3 minutes, or until dark golden brown. Turn steaks and cook for an additional 2 to 3 minutes on remaining side.

5 Serve warm alongside fresh or steamed greens, or another vegetable side.

Variation: To make **Paprika Cauliflower Steaks,** simply replace ras el hanout and cayenne pepper with 1 tablespoon smoked paprika, 1 teaspoon ground cumin, and 2 teaspoons granulated garlic.

EACH SERVING HAS:

Calories **171**   Total Fat **8g**   Carbohydrate **22g**   Protein **8g**

Toasty oven-roasted **spring peas** and **pearl onions** are tossed in **fresh mint** and a **splash of lemon,** and topped with paper-thin slices of **salty, dry-cured ham.**

Spring Peas and Pearl Onions with Mint

 6 CUPS   5 MINUTES   20 MINUTES   1½ CUPS

INGREDIENTS

2 TB. extra-virgin olive oil

8 small pearl onions, quartered

4 cups fresh spring peas, stems trimmed

¼ tsp. sea salt

⅛ tsp. freshly ground black pepper

10 mint leaves, chopped

1 tsp. fresh lemon juice

½ oz. (14g) serrano ham or prosciutto, finely chopped (optional)

METHOD

1 Preheat the oven to 450°F (230°C).

2 Cut a piece of parchment paper to line the bottom of a large rimmed baking sheet (or use a silicone sheet liner).

3 In a large bowl, toss extra-virgin olive oil, pearl onions, spring peas, sea salt, and black pepper until vegetables are fully coated. Spread vegetables out evenly on the sheet.

4 Bake for 8 minutes. Remove the sheet from the oven, stir with a wooden spoon, and return to the oven for 8 to 10 minutes, or until vegetables are tender.

5 Toss roasted vegetables with mint and lemon juice, and top with serrano ham (if using). Serve warm.

Variation: If you'd like to skip any extra nitrates that can be naturally found or added in cured pork products, feel free to substitute ¼ cup sliced and pitted black olives instead to still get that salty component.

EACH SERVING HAS:

Calories **177**   Total Fat **7g**   Carbohydrate **21g**   Protein **8g**

Lush green chard leaves and colorful stems are punched up with **browned garlic** and **fiery crushed red pepper flakes.**

Braised **Chard**

 2 CUPS   **10 MINUTES**   **5 MINUTES**   **½ CUP**

INGREDIENTS

1 lb. (450g) Swiss chard

1 TB. extra-virgin olive oil

2 garlic cloves, thinly sliced

1 tsp. crushed red pepper flakes

¼ tsp. sea salt

METHOD

1 Using a knife, carefully separate Swiss chard stems from leaves. Coarsely chop leaves and finely slice stems.

2 Heat a large skillet over medium-high heat. When the skillet is hot, add extra-virgin olive oil and wait 30 seconds.

3 Add garlic and Swiss chard stems, and sauté, stirring frequently, for 30 seconds to 1 minute, or until garlic is very aromatic and beginning to turn golden brown.

4 Add Swiss chard leaves, crushed red pepper flakes, and sea salt. Continue to sauté, stirring frequently, for 1 minute, or until leaves wilt.

5 Remove from heat and serve immediately.

Variation: This recipe is fantastic with any type of seasonal dark, leafy green. Mustard greens, lacinato kale, beet greens, or carrot tops are all highly recommended substitutions for Swiss chard. You may need to cook certain tougher greens longer than tender Swiss chard leaves, however.

This recipe is so easy and versatile, you may find yourself using it as a side for grilled meats, the base of a unique salad, or a bed for an Olive Oil–Fried Egg.

EACH SERVING HAS:

Calories **60**   Total Fat **4g**   Carbohydrate **5g**   Protein **2g**

seafood

Seafood can be a bit intimidating for a beginning cook. These recipes will have you cooking like a pro in no time, with instructions on everything from choosing and cleaning live shellfish to properly searing fish so it doesn't fall apart in the pan. With flavorful fresh herbs, sauces, and marinades, it's easy to make seafood a fast and convenient part of your weekly meal plan.

Charred calamari is marinated in **garlic, lemon,** and **bright ground cumin,** with a spicy pop of **Calabrian chiles.**

Calamari with Cumin

 2 CUPS 2 TO 6 HOURS 6 MINUTES ½ CUP

INGREDIENTS

1 lb. (450g) fresh calamari (tubes and tentacles), cleaned

2 TB. plus 1 tsp. extra-virgin olive oil

1 TB. ground cumin

4 Calabrian chiles, minced

2 cloves garlic, minced

2 TB. fresh lemon juice

½ tsp. coarse sea salt

2 TB. fresh oregano leaves

METHOD

1 In a medium nonreactive bowl or resealable bag, combine calamari, 2 tablespoons extra-virgin olive oil, cumin, Calabrian chiles, garlic, 1 tablespoon lemon juice, and ¼ teaspoon sea salt.

2 Cover (or seal the bag) and refrigerate for 2 to 6 hours. Shortly before mealtime, drain any excess liquid from calamari.

3 Heat a large cast-iron skillet over high heat. Add remaining 1 teaspoon extra-virgin olive oil and wait 30 seconds.

4 Spread calamari evenly in the bottom of the hot skillet and cook for 2 to 3 minutes, or until edges are charred. Turn calamari and cook for 2 to 3 minutes on the remaining side.

5 Remove calamari from the skillet. Sprinkle with remaining 1 tablespoon lemon juice, remaining ¼ teaspoon sea salt, and fresh oregano leaves to serve.

There's no need for an outdoor grill to enjoy deliciously charred seafood. The tender tentacles of calamari crisp up nicely in a piping-hot cast-iron skillet.

EACH SERVING HAS:

| Calories 192 | Total Fat 14g | Carbohydrate 3g | Protein 15g |

Flaky **tuna steak** is served alongside a crisp salad of **fresh orange slices, crunchy raw fennel,** and **olives,** with a **whole-grain mustard vinaigrette.**

Tuna Steak with Orange and Fennel Salad

 2 STEAKS   **15 MINUTES**   **6 MINUTES**   **1 STEAK**

INGREDIENTS

2 (4-oz.; 110g) tuna steaks

¼ tsp. sea salt

½ tsp. freshly ground black pepper

1 medium fennel bulb, trimmed and halved

4 tsp. extra-virgin olive oil

1 tsp. fresh lemon juice

1 tsp. whole-grain mustard

1 tsp. fresh dill weed, chopped

1 medium orange, peeled and chopped

½ cup kalamata olives

METHOD

1 Season both sides of tuna steaks lightly with sea salt and ¼ teaspoon black pepper.

2 Cut fennel into ¼-inch (.5cm) slices, removing tough inner core as you slice.

3 In a small bowl, whisk 2 teaspoons extra-virgin olive oil, lemon juice, whole-grain mustard, dill, and remaining ¼ teaspoon black pepper until fully combined to make dressing. Alternately, place ingredients into a small Mason jar, cover tightly with a lid, and shake vigorously until fully combined.

4 Place a medium skillet over medium heat. When the skillet is hot, add remaining 2 teaspoons extra-virgin olive oil and wait 30 seconds.

5 Place tuna steaks in hot oil. Cook for 1 to 3 minutes per side, until surfaces are golden brown and center is cooked as desired.

6 Meanwhile, combine fennel, orange, kalamata olives, and dressing in a medium bowl. Toss until coated.

7 Serve tuna steaks over orange and fennel salad.

EACH SERVING HAS:

Calories **320**   Total Fat **12g**   Carbohydrate **26g**   Protein **29g**

Baked **whole branzino** is stuffed with **gremolata:** a bright combination of **zingy lemon zest,** ample amounts of **garlic,** and **fresh parsley.**

Baked Branzino with
Gremolata

| 1 FISH | 15 MINUTES | 25 MINUTES | ½ FISH |

INGREDIENTS

Zest of 2 medium lemons (about 4 tsp.)

5 garlic cloves, minced

1 cup flat-leaf parsley, finely chopped

2 tsp. capers, rinsed

¾ tsp. sea salt

1 whole branzino, about 1 lb. (450g), cleaned

1 TB. extra-virgin olive oil

¼ tsp. freshly ground black pepper

METHOD

1 Preheat the oven to 475°F (250°C).

2 To make gremolata, in a small bowl, combine lemon zest, garlic, flat-leaf parsley, capers, and ¼ teaspoon sea salt.

3 Stuff cavity of branzino with gremolata. Place stuffed branzino on a parchment-lined baking sheet.

4 Drizzle branzino with extra-virgin olive oil and sprinkle with remaining ½ teaspoon sea salt and black pepper.

5 Bake for 20 to 25 minutes, or until eyes have turned opaque white and flesh just under skin flakes easily with a fork.

6 Remove branzino skin, head, and bones before serving.

Variation: To make **Baked Branzino with Fennel,** simply fill branzino cavity with ½ medium fennel bulb, ½ lemon, and 2 garlic cloves, all thinly sliced, instead of gremolata.

EACH SERVING HAS:

| Calories **306** | Total Fat **12g** | Carbohydrate **5g** | Protein **44g** |

Delicate sole fillets are paired with a salad of **sweet heirloom tomatoes,** buttery Castelvetrano olives, and a pop of **toasted pine nuts.**

Sole with Fresh Tomato Salad

 2 FILLETS   **15 MINUTES**   **5 MINUTES**   **1 FILLET**

INGREDIENTS

- 2 (4-oz.; 110g) sole fillets
- ½ tsp. sea salt
- ¼ tsp. freshly ground black pepper
- 2 TB. extra-virgin olive oil
- ½ lb. (225g) heirloom tomatoes, diced
- ½ cup Castelvetrano olives
- 2 TB. fresh basil, chopped
- 1 TB. fresh lemon juice
- 2 TB. toasted pine nuts

METHOD

1 Season both sides of sole fillets lightly with ¼ teaspoon sea salt and black pepper.

2 Place a medium skillet over medium-high heat. When the skillet is hot, add 1 tablespoon extra-virgin olive oil and wait 30 seconds.

3 Place fillets in hot oil. Cook for 1 to 2 minutes per side, until surfaces are golden brown and centers flake easily with a fork.

4 Meanwhile, in a large bowl, combine heirloom tomatoes, Castelvetrano olives, basil, lemon juice, toasted pine nuts, remaining ¼ teaspoon sea salt, and remaining 1 tablespoon extra-virgin olive oil. Toss to coat.

5 Serve sole fillets over fresh tomato salad.

This recipe is best in the height of summer, when heirloom tomatoes have fully ripened in the sun and are bursting with natural sweetness and flavor. For other times of the year, try using sweet cherry or grape tomatoes as a substitute.

EACH SERVING HAS:

Calories **345**   Total Fat **25g**   Carbohydrate **16g**   Protein **20g**

Crispy vegetables are marinated in a **cilantro, parsley,** and **paprika dressing,** and served alongside **tender pan-fried salmon fillets.**

Salmon with Chermoula-Marinated Vegetables

SALMON

 2 FILLETS   **5 MINUTES**   **10 MINUTES**   **1 FILLET**

INGREDIENTS

2 (6-oz.; 170g) boneless salmon fillets, about 1½ in. (3.75cm) thick

½ tsp. sea salt

¼ tsp. freshly ground black pepper

2 tsp. extra-virgin olive oil

METHOD

1 Preheat the oven to 450°F (230°C).

2 Sprinkle both sides of salmon fillets with sea salt and black pepper. Set aside until the oven reaches the proper temperature.

3 Heat a medium skillet over medium-high heat. When the skillet is hot, add extra-virgin olive oil and wait 30 seconds. (If your cooking space isn't ventilated well, you may want to use tallow or avocado oil instead of olive oil to help cut down on extra smoke.)

4 Place salmon fillets, skin side up, in the hot skillet. Cook for 1 minute, or until a golden crust forms and fish easily releases from the skillet. If fish sticks to the pan, cook a few more seconds until it cleanly releases when lifted with a metal spatula.

5 Turn salmon fillets and cook for 1 minute. Place the hot skillet in the oven and finish cooking for 6 to 8 minutes, or until salmon is cooked to your liking.

6 Serve with Chermoula-Marinated Vegetables.

EACH SERVING HAS:

Calories **280**   Total Fat **14g**   Carbohydrate **0g**   Protein **36g**

CHERMOULA-MARINATED VEGETABLES

 8 CUPS   4 TO 24 HOURS, 15 MINUTES   NONE   2 CUPS

INGREDIENTS

1½ cups cilantro

½ cup flat-leaf parsley

6 garlic cloves, sliced

1 tsp. ground cumin

1 tsp. smoked paprika

¾ tsp. sea salt

¼ tsp. cayenne pepper

½ cup extra-virgin olive oil

2 TB. lemon juice

1 red bell pepper, seeded and sliced

1 yellow zucchini or summer squash, trimmed and thinly sliced

¼ small red cabbage, thinly sliced (about 1 cup)

2 cups broccoli or cauliflower florets

1 medium carrot, peeled and thinly sliced

METHOD

1 To make chermoula, in a food processor, combine cilantro, flat-leaf parsley, garlic, cumin, smoked paprika, sea salt, cayenne pepper, extra-virgin olive oil, and lemon juice.

2 Pulse for 30 seconds, or until a paste forms. Taste and adjust seasonings, if desired.

3 In a medium bowl, combine chermoula, red bell pepper, yellow zucchini, red cabbage, broccoli, and carrot, and toss until vegetables are fully coated with dressing.

4 Cover and refrigerate for 4 to 24 hours. Serve cold with Salmon.

EACH SERVING HAS:

Calories **325**   Total Fat **29g**   Carbohydrate **14g**   Protein **4g**

Succulent prawns flavored with **garlic** are gently sautéed and served with a warmly spiced salad of **grated carrot** and **sweet dried currants**.

Garlic Ginger Prawns with
Spiced Carrot-Currant Salad

GARLIC GINGER PRAWNS

 16 PRAWNS 35 MINUTES 5 MINUTES 4 PRAWNS

INGREDIENTS

¼ cup extra-virgin olive oil

4 garlic cloves, minced

2 tsp. fresh ginger root, grated

16 large prawns

Sea salt

METHOD

1 In a medium bowl, combine extra-virgin olive oil, garlic, and ginger. Add prawns and toss to coat. Cover the bowl and refrigerate for at least 30 minutes.

2 Shortly before mealtime, place a large skillet over medium-high heat.

3 When the skillet is hot, add prawns with remaining garlic and ginger–infused oil. Sauté, stirring frequently, for 2 to 4 minutes, or until prawns are bright pink.

4 Remove from heat, season with sea salt to taste, and serve immediately with Spiced Carrot-Currant Salad.

EACH SERVING HAS:

Calories **265**   Total Fat **19g**   Carbohydrate **1g**   Protein **19g**

SPICED CARROT-CURRANT SALAD

 4 CUPS 15 MINUTES NONE 1 CUP

INGREDIENTS

4 tsp. extra-virgin olive oil

¼ cup fresh orange juice

2 tsp. ras el hanout

¼ tsp. sea salt

1½ lb. (680g) carrots, grated (about 4 cups)

½ cup dried currants

½ cup fresh cilantro, chopped

½ cup pistachios

METHOD

1 In a small bowl, whisk extra-virgin olive oil, orange juice, ras el hanout, and sea salt until fully combined to make dressing. Alternately, place ingredients into a small Mason jar, cover tightly with a lid, and shake vigorously until fully combined.

2 In a salad bowl, combine carrots, currants, cilantro, pistachios, and dressing. Toss to coat completely.

3 Serve over Garlic Ginger Prawns.

EACH SERVING HAS:

Calories **262**   Total Fat **12g**   Carbohydrate **36g**   Protein **6g**

Tender whitefish, simmered in fragrant spices and hearty vegetables, is topped with crunchy toasted almonds and fresh cilantro.

Whitefish Tagine with
Tomatoes

 8 CUPS   15 MINUTES   40 MINUTES   2 CUPS

INGREDIENTS

1 large eggplant, cut into 1-in. (2.5cm) cubes

3 TB. extra-virgin olive oil (plus more for rubbing fish)

1 lb. (450g) skinless, boneless whitefish fillets

1 tsp. sea salt

1 small shallot, minced

2 garlic cloves, sliced

1 tsp. ground cinnamon

1 tsp. ground cumin

1 tsp. ground ginger

½ tsp. turmeric

¼ tsp. freshly ground black pepper

1 (15-oz.; 420g) can diced tomatoes, with juice

1 medium zucchini, diced

1 medium carrot, peeled and diced

2 cups small cauliflower florets

2 TB. capers

2 TB. fresh cilantro, chopped

2 TB. slivered almonds, lightly toasted

EACH SERVING HAS:

Calories 280
Total Fat 12g
Carbohydrate 19g
Protein 5g

METHOD

1 Rub eggplant cubes with a bit of extra-virgin olive oil to keep from browning. Set aside. Sprinkle whitefish fillets with ½ teaspoon sea salt. Place in the refrigerator for later use.

2 Heat a large Dutch oven or braiser over medium-high heat. When it's hot, add extra-virgin olive oil and wait 30 seconds.

3 Add shallot and garlic, and sauté, stirring frequently, for 2 to 3 minutes, or until shallot is slightly translucent and garlic is golden brown.

4 Add cinnamon, cumin, ginger, turmeric, and black pepper. Stir, and cook for 30 seconds. Reduce heat to low.

5 Add tomatoes (with juice), eggplant, zucchini, carrot, cauliflower, and remaining ½ teaspoon sea salt. Stir, cover, and simmer for 30 minutes.

6 Taste and adjust sea salt, if needed. Add capers and whitefish fillets. Cover and simmer for 2 to 3 minutes, or until fish flakes with a fork.

7 Garnish with fresh cilantro and slivered almonds to serve.

Sweet roasted bell peppers with **salty anchovies** and **buttery Castelvetrano** olives make the perfect light lunch paired with **grain-free bread** or crackers.

Roasted Peppers with
Anchovies and Castelvetranos

 2 CUPS   **5 MINUTES**   **20 MINUTES**   **½ CUP**

INGREDIENTS

6 roasted red bell peppers (about 1½ cups), sliced

2 oz. (55g) oil-packed anchovies, drained

2 garlic cloves, minced

½ cup pitted Castelvetrano olives, coarsely chopped

3 TB. flat-leaf parsley, minced

1 TB. extra-virgin olive oil

¼ tsp. freshly ground black pepper

2 tsp. fresh lemon juice

METHOD

1 Preheat the oven to 425°F (220°C).

2 Place red bell peppers, anchovies, garlic, Castelvetrano olives, flat-leaf parsley, extra-virgin olive oil, and black pepper in a shallow baking dish.

3 Bake, uncovered, for 15 to 20 minutes, or until anchovies crisp slightly on top.

4 Sprinkle with lemon juice and serve with Grain-Free Flatbread, Olive and Onion Focaccia, Nut and Seed Crackers, or any other Paleo bread.

To roast your own red bell peppers, simply cut each pepper in half, place skin side up on a metal baking sheet, and broil on high until skins are charred and black. Transfer peppers immediately to a large resealable plastic bag, close the bag, and let steam for 15 minutes. Once steamed, peel skins from peppers, and cut away stems and white membranes.

EACH SERVING HAS:

Calories **182**   Total Fat **14g**   Carbohydrate **7g**   Protein **5g**

Hearty fillets of **salmon**, spiced with **za'atar**, are baked on a bed of **sweet butternut squash couscous** and drizzled with a **tangy tahini yogurt sauce**.

Salmon with Butternut Squash Couscous

 2 FILLETS   **15 MINUTES**   **30 MINUTES**   **1 FILLET**

INGREDIENTS

1 small butternut squash (about 2 lb.; 1kg)

4 tsp. extra-virgin olive oil

¾ tsp. sea salt

2 garlic cloves, minced

1 TB. preserved lemon peel, thinly sliced

2 TB. flat-leaf parsley, chopped

½ medium red onion, thinly sliced

2 (6-oz.; 170g) boneless salmon fillets, about 1½ in. (3.75cm) thick

1 TB. za'atar

2 TB. tahini

¼ cup full-fat yogurt or coconut yogurt

1 TB. fresh lemon juice

1 TB. water

METHOD

1 Preheat the oven to 375°F (190°C).

2 Trim stem and blossom end off butternut squash and cut in half lengthwise. Using a sturdy spoon, scoop out seeds and discard. Cut each half into half again to make quarters.

3 Using a sharp knife, carefully trim off butternut squash peel on each quarter. Cut each peeled quarter into thirds and place in a food processor. Pulse for 30 to 45 seconds, or until a coarse couscous consistency forms.

4 Transfer squash to a medium roasting pan or Dutch oven, along with 2 teaspoons extra-virgin olive oil, ½ teaspoon sea salt, garlic, preserved lemon peel, flat-leaf parsley, and red onion. Mix with a wooden spoon and spread out in the bottom of the pan.

5 Sprinkle salmon fillets with za'atar, remaining 2 teaspoons extra-virgin olive oil, and remaining ¼ teaspoon sea salt. Place fillets side by side, on top of vegetables, in the pan.

6 Bake, uncovered, for 25 to 30 minutes, or until vegetables are tender and salmon flakes easily with a fork.

7 Meanwhile, in a small bowl, combine tahini, full-fat yogurt, lemon juice, and water. Drizzle over cooked salmon and vegetables to serve.

Variation: This recipe can also be made with grated sweet potatoes or yams instead of butternut squash.

EACH SERVING HAS:

| Calories 643 | Total Fat 24g | Carbohydrate 72g | Protein 49g |

Buttery, seared sea scallops with a saffron-infused cauliflower rice are spruced up with fresh tomatoes, piquillo peppers, and thin slices of serrano ham.

Seared Scallops with Saffron-Cauliflower Rice

SEARED SCALLOPS

 4 SCALLOPS   **1 MINUTE**   **5 MINUTES**   **2 SCALLOPS**

INGREDIENTS

4 large fresh sea scallops, rinsed

2 TB. extra-virgin olive oil

¼ tsp. sea salt

METHOD

1 Gently dry sea scallops on both sides with paper towels.

2 Place a medium skillet over high heat. When the skillet is hot, add extra-virgin oil and wait 30 seconds. Oil should smoke slightly.

3 Add sea scallops to the skillet (it should sizzle loudly). Cook for 30 seconds to 1 minute, or until a deep golden crust forms. Turn sea scallops and repeat on other side.

4 Sprinkle with sea salt and serve over Saffron-Cauliflower Rice.

EACH SERVING HAS:

Calories **228**   Total Fat **15g**   Carbohydrate **6g**   Protein **19g**

SAFFRON-CAULIFLOWER RICE

 3 CUPS   **5 MINUTES**   **15 MINUTES**   **1½ CUPS**

INGREDIENTS

12 saffron threads

3 cups cauliflower florets (about ½ medium head)

1 TB. extra-virgin olive oil

1 spring onion (or 2 scallions), white and light green parts only, thinly sliced

1 cup cherry or small heirloom tomatoes, quartered or diced

2 piquillo peppers or 1 roasted bell pepper, thinly sliced

½ tsp. sea salt

¼ tsp. black pepper

2 tsp. fresh lemon juice

2 thin slices serrano ham, sliced (optional)

METHOD

1 Place saffron threads in 2 tablespoons warm water. Let sit for 5 minutes.

2 Place cauliflower florets into a food processor and pulse for 15 to 20 seconds, or until a ricelike consistency forms.

3 Place a large skillet over medium-high heat. When the skillet is hot, add extra-virgin olive oil and wait 30 seconds.

4 Add spring onion and sauté, stirring frequently, for 30 seconds, or until golden brown. Add cherry tomatoes, piquillo peppers, riced cauliflower, sea salt, and black pepper, and stir for 2 to 3 minutes.

5 Add saffron threads and residual water. Cover and let steam for 1 minute.

6 To serve, sprinkle lemon juice and serrano ham slices (if using) over it and place Seared Scallops on top.

EACH SERVING HAS:

Calories **130**

Total Fat **8g**

Carbohydrate **15g**

Protein **4g**

Fresh mussels are lightly steamed in **garlic** and **white wine** and served alongside **crisp celeriac fries.**

Garlic Mussels and
Celeriac Fries

GARLIC MUSSELS

 32 MUSSELS   **5 MINUTES**   **8 MINUTES**   **8 MUSSELS**

INGREDIENTS

1 TB. extra-virgin olive oil

4 garlic cloves, minced

32 live mussels (about 2 lb.; 1kg), cleaned and de-bearded

½ cup dry white wine

½ tsp. sea salt

1 TB. fresh lemon juice

¼ cup fresh flat-leaf parsley, chopped

METHOD

1 Place a large skillet over medium-high heat. When the skillet is hot, add extra-virgin olive oil and wait 30 seconds.

2 Add garlic and sauté, stirring constantly, for 1 to 2 minutes, or until golden brown.

3 Add mussels and dry white wine. Cover immediately and simmer for 4 to 5 minutes, or until mussels open.

4 Discard any unopened mussels. Add sea salt, lemon juice, and flat-leaf parsley, and toss gently to combine. Serve immediately with Celeriac Fries.

EACH SERVING HAS:

Calories **281**   Total Fat **16g**   Carbohydrate **8g**   Protein **11g**

CELERIAC FRIES

 4 CUPS   **10 MINUTES**   **35 MINUTES**   **1 CUP**

INGREDIENTS

2 large celery roots, trimmed and peeled

2 TB. extra-virgin olive oil

2 tsp. dried thyme

½ tsp. sea salt (or more, if desired)

½ tsp. freshly ground black pepper

METHOD

1 Cut celery roots into ¼-inch (.5cm) slices. Cut each slice into ¼-inch (.5cm) strips to make "fries."

2 Fill a 3-quart (3L) pot with 6 cups water and bring to a boil over high heat.

3 When water is boiling, add celery root fries and boil, uncovered, for 2 minutes.

4 Meanwhile, preheat the oven to 425°F (220°C).

5 Drain celery roots. Add extra-virgin olive oil, thyme, sea salt, and black pepper, and toss to coat.

6 Spread celery roots on a rimmed metal baking sheet. Bake for 25 to 30 minutes, or until crisped. Serve alongside Garlic Mussels.

EACH SERVING HAS:

Calories **148**   Total Fat **7g**   Carbohydrate **18g**   Protein **0g**

poultry

Poultry will never be dull again with this variety of recipes using chicken, turkey, duck, and game hen. With the right spices, marinades, and rubs, this lean protein will explode with flavor. This chapter teaches you techniques for preparing boneless, skinless cuts, as well as more flavorful bone-in, skin-on choices.

Chicken thighs are rubbed with a **robust blend of paprika, cardamom, garlic, and ginger,** and roasted atop **tender broccolini.**

Paprika-Rubbed Chicken with Broccolini

 4 PIECES　　 **10 MINUTES**　　 **45 MINUTES**　　 **1 PIECE**

INGREDIENTS

1 tsp. smoked paprika

1 tsp. cardamom

½ tsp. granulated garlic

½ tsp. ground ginger

¾ tsp. sea salt

½ tsp. freshly ground black pepper

4 large chicken thighs (1½ lb.; 680g), bone in and skin on

¾ lb. (340g) broccolini, trimmed

3 tsp. extra-virgin olive oil

¼ cup toasted hazelnuts, chopped

EACH SERVING HAS:

Calories 479

Total Fat 35g

Carbohydrate 9g

Protein 31g

METHOD

1 Preheat the oven to 375°F (190°C).

2 In a small bowl, combine smoked paprika, cardamom, garlic, ginger, ½ teaspoon sea salt, and black pepper.

3 Using clean hands, rub all sides of each chicken thigh with spice mixture. Be sure to also carefully reach under skin and rub flesh underneath with spices.

4 In a large mixing bowl, toss broccolini in 1 teaspoon extra-virgin olive oil and remaining ¼ teaspoon sea salt.

5 Heat a large ovenproof skillet or Dutch oven over medium-high heat. When the skillet is hot, add remaining 2 teaspoons extra-virgin olive oil and wait 30 seconds, or until the skillet begins to smoke lightly. Reduce heat to medium.

6 Place chicken thighs in the skillet, skin side down. Brown for 2 to 3 minutes per side, or until dark golden brown. Remove from the skillet.

7 Place broccolini in the bottom of the hot skillet. Add chicken thighs on top, skin side up. Place the skillet in the oven and bake for 25 to 35 minutes, or until chicken reaches an internal temperature of 165°F (75°C).

8 Top with toasted hazelnuts to serve.

Spicy harissa-glazed **wings** are sweetened with a **hint of honey** and brightened with **fresh orange zest.**

Orange and Harissa–Glazed **Chicken Wings**

 16 PIECES   **1 HOUR, 15 MINUTES**   **50 MINUTES**   **4 PIECES**

INGREDIENTS

- 8 whole chicken wings
- 1 TB. extra-virgin olive oil
- ½ tsp. sea salt
- 2 TB. raw honey
- 1½ tsp. fresh orange zest
- 1 tsp. harissa
- ½ tsp. granulated garlic powder
- 1 TB. fresh cilantro, chopped

METHOD

1 To separate whole chicken wings, first identify drumettes (small leg bones), two-bone middle sections (called *flats*), and tiny wing tips.

2 Find joint between drumettes and flats. Using a sharp knife, cut directly through joint separation. Do the same between flats and wing tips. Repeat for all wings, and discard wing tips (or save for stock).

3 Rinse drumettes and flats with water to remove any bone fragments. Pat dry with paper towels.

4 Line a rimmed metal baking sheet with foil. Place a metal cooling rack on top, and spread chicken pieces evenly on the rack. Place in the refrigerator, uncovered, for 60 minutes to fully dry chicken skin.

5 After chicken is done drying, preheat the oven to 400°F (200°C).

6 Remove wings from the rack and, in a medium bowl, toss in extra-virgin olive oil and sea salt. Place on the rack again, and bake for 35 to 45 minutes, or until skin is golden and crisped.

7 Meanwhile, to make glaze, combine raw honey, orange zest, harissa, and garlic powder in a small bowl.

8 When chicken is done, brush with glaze and bake for 4 to 5 minutes, or until glaze is shiny and caramelized. Garnish with fresh cilantro to serve.

EACH SERVING HAS:

Calories	Total Fat	Carbohydrate	Protein
266	17g	9g	18g

Succulent seasoned duck breast is served on a vibrant salad of radicchio, pomegranate, oranges, and **fresh mint,** with an **orange juice–Dijon vinaigrette.**

Spiced Duck with Raddichio and Pomegranate

 6 SLICES AND 2 SALADS   **15 MINUTES**   **8 MINUTES**   **3 SLICES AND 1 SALAD**

INGREDIENTS

- 6 tsp. extra-virgin olive oil
- 1 TB. fresh orange juice
- 2 tsp. shallot, minced
- 1 tsp. Dijon mustard
- 1 tsp. raw honey
- ½ tsp. sea salt
- ¼ tsp. freshly ground black pepper
- 1 small boneless duck breast (about 8 oz.; 225g), skin on
- ½ tsp. ras el hanout
- 1 medium head radicchio, coarsely chopped
- 1 small orange, peeled and segmented
- ½ cup pomegranate seeds
- ¼ cup fresh mint leaves
- ½ cup pecans, chopped

METHOD

1 In a small bowl, whisk 5 teaspoons extra-virgin olive oil, orange juice, shallot, Dijon mustard, raw honey, ¼ teaspoon sea salt, and black pepper until fully combined to make dressing. Alternately, place ingredients into a small Mason jar, cover tightly with a lid, and shake vigorously until fully combined.

2 Sprinkle skin side of duck breast with remaining ¼ teaspoon sea salt and ras el hanout.

3 Place a small skillet over medium-high heat. When the skillet is hot, add remaining 1 teaspoon extra-virgin olive oil and wait 30 seconds.

4 Place duck breast skin side down in the skillet. Immediately lower temperature to medium-low. Cook duck for 2 to 3 minutes, or until skin is a deep golden brown and crisp. Turn duck breast and finish cooking to desired temperature, about 3 to 5 minutes.

5 Meanwhile, in a medium bowl, combine radicchio, orange segments, pomegranate seeds, mint, pecans, and dressing. Toss to coat.

6 When duck is cooked through, cut breast into 6 slices. Divide salad into bowls and top with duck breast slices to serve.

EACH SERVING HAS:

Calories 561	Total Fat 37g	Carbohydrate 30g	Protein 32g

Crisped chicken thighs are simmered atop **cauliflower rice** and **sofrito:** an aromatic blend of **sautéed onions, garlic, red bell pepper,** and **tomato.**

Chicken Sofrito with
Cauliflower Rice

 6 THIGHS AND 6 CUPS RICE   **20 MINUTES**   **45 MINUTES**   **1 THIGH AND 1 CUP RICE**

INGREDIENTS

- 2 tsp. sea salt
- 2 tsp. sweet paprika
- 6 chicken thighs, bone in and skin on
- 1 TB. extra-virgin olive oil
- 1 medium yellow onion, diced
- 4 garlic cloves, sliced
- 1 jalapeño, seeded and minced
- 1 medium red bell pepper, seeded and diced
- 1 TB. fresh thyme leaves
- ¼ tsp. cayenne pepper (optional)
- 1 large tomato, diced
- 1 cup chicken stock or broth
- 1 medium head cauliflower, riced
- Juice of 1 medium lemon (about 2 TB.)
- ½ cup slivered almonds, toasted

METHOD

1 Preheat the oven to 375°F (190°C). In a small bowl, mix sea salt and sweet paprika. Spread mixture on skin side of each chicken thigh.

2 Place a large cast-iron skillet or Dutch oven over medium-high heat. When the skillet is hot, add extra-virgin olive oil and wait 30 seconds.

3 Place chicken thighs, seasoned side down, in hot oil. Cook for 2 to 3 minutes, or until skins are nicely browned. Turn and repeat on other side. Remove chicken from the skillet and set aside.

4 Add yellow onion to the hot skillet and sauté, stirring frequently, for 3 minutes. Add garlic and continue to sauté for 1 minute, or until onion is slightly translucent and garlic is fragrant and golden.

5 Add jalapeño, red bell pepper, thyme, cayenne pepper (if using), and tomato, and cook for another 5 to 6 minutes, or until most of liquid in the bottom of the skillet cooks off.

6 Add chicken stock, riced cauliflower, lemon juice, and slivered almonds, and stir to combine. Place chicken thighs, skin side up, on top of cauliflower mixture.

7 Bake, uncovered, for 20 to 25 minutes, or until chicken is cooked through. Serve.

EACH SERVING HAS:

| Calories 374 | Total Fat 23g | Carbohydrate 13g | Protein 30g |

Juicy **roast chicken** is baked with **garlic, lemon,** and **sage,** and served alongside a **hearty root vegetable assortment.**

Whole Roast Chicken
with Root Vegetables

 1 WHOLE CHICKEN   40 MINUTES   1 HOUR, 30 MINUTES   ⅙ CHICKEN

INGREDIENTS

1 (5-lb.; 2.25kg) whole chicken

4 TB. extra-virgin olive oil

1½ tsp. sea salt

1 tsp. freshly ground black pepper

10 fresh sage leaves, finely chopped

10 garlic cloves, crushed

1 lemon, quartered

1 large sweet yellow onion, halved and sliced

2 large sweet potatoes or yams, diced

1 large celery root, peeled and diced

1 medium rutabaga, peeled and diced

2 medium carrots, peeled and diced

METHOD

1 Preheat the oven to 425°F (220°C).

2 Remove any giblets or plastic wrappings from cavity of chicken. Rinse cavity (trying not to get too much water on skin), and pat dry with a paper towel. Set chicken, breast side up, in a large roasting pan.

3 Rub 2 tablespoons extra-virgin olive oil all over outside of chicken and between skin and flesh. Sprinkle chicken with 1 teaspoon sea salt and ½ teaspoon black pepper.

4 Stuff chicken cavity with sage, garlic, and lemon, and let rest on the counter for 20 minutes. Place the pan in the oven and bake for 30 minutes.

5 Meanwhile, in a large mixing bowl, place sweet yellow onion, sweet potatoes, celery root, rutabaga, carrots, remaining 2 tablespoons extra-virgin olive oil, remaining ½ teaspoon sea salt, and remaining ½ teaspoon black pepper. Stir until vegetables are fully coated.

6 After 30 minutes, remove chicken from the oven. Transfer root vegetables to the roasting pan (you may need to lift chicken out and place it on top of vegetables). Leave all drippings in the pan, and make sure vegetables don't cover chicken.

7 Return chicken and vegetables to the oven, and bake for 45 to 60 minutes, or until chicken reaches an internal temperature of 165°F (75°C).

8 Remove from the oven, and let chicken rest for 15 minutes before slicing and serving with vegetables.

EACH SERVING HAS:

Calories 678   Total Fat 33g   Carbohydrate 15g   Protein 78g

Juicy grilled chicken breasts are marinated in **fresh citrus, ginger,** and **garlic,** and served on a bed of **peppery arugula.**

Citrus Grilled Chicken
with Greens

 6 CUPS   4 TO 8 HOURS, 15 MINUTES   20 MINUTES   3 CUPS

INGREDIENTS

¼ cup fresh orange juice

2 TB. fresh lemon juice

2 TB. fresh lime juice

1 TB. extra-virgin olive oil

1 tsp. freshly grated ginger root

2 garlic cloves, minced

1 lb. (450g) boneless, skinless chicken breasts

¾ tsp. sea salt

¼ tsp. freshly ground black pepper

6 cups baby arugula or mixed greens

½ cup nuts of choice, toasted and chopped

METHOD

1 In a medium glass or plastic container (or a large zipper-lock plastic bag), combine orange juice, lemon juice, lime juice, extra-virgin olive oil, ginger root, and garlic.

2 Place chicken breasts in the container, cover, and shake to fully coat. Refrigerate for 4 to 8 hours.

3 Shortly before mealtime, remove chicken from the refrigerator. Drain chicken from liquid (don't discard liquid) and place on a plate.

4 Preheat the grill to medium-high.

5 Meanwhile, in a small saucepan over medium-high heat, place reserved marinade. Bring to a boil for 5 minutes. Remove from heat to cool, and season with ¼ teaspoon sea salt (or more, if desired).

6 Sprinkle both sides of chicken breasts with remaining ½ teaspoon sea salt and black pepper.

7 When the grill is hot, place seasoned chicken on the grill. Cook, turning once, for 10 to 15 minutes, or until chicken reaches an internal temperature of 165°F (75°C).

8 To serve, slice chicken into thin strips. Divide baby arugula into 4 serving bowls and add chicken to each. Drizzle each bowl with boiled marinade as a dressing or sauce. Sprinkle with toasted nuts.

EACH SERVING HAS:

| Calories 490 | Total Fat 32g | Carbohydrate 12g | Protein 43g |

Lean turkey kebabs—spiced up with **garlic, coriander,** and **cumin**—are served alongside **bright vegetable kebabs** and a **tahini yogurt sauce.**

Turkey Kebabs with
Zucchini and Tahini

 16 KEBABS   **15 TO 45 MINUTES**   **6 MINUTES**   **4 KEBABS**

INGREDIENTS

2 medium zucchini, trimmed and cut into ½-in. (1.25cm) slices

24 cherry tomatoes

¾ tsp. sea salt

4 tsp. extra-virgin olive oil

1 tsp. granulated garlic

1 tsp. ground coriander

½ tsp. ground cumin

2 green onions, thinly sliced (white and light green parts only)

1 large egg, beaten

1 lb. (450g) ground turkey

2 TB. tahini

¼ cup full-fat yogurt or coconut yogurt

2 tsp. fresh lemon juice

1 TB. water

2 TB. fresh oregano, chopped

METHOD

1 In a medium bowl, toss zucchini and cherry tomatoes with ¼ teaspoon sea salt and 2 teaspoons extra-virgin olive oil. Set aside.

2 In a second medium bowl, combine remaining ½ teaspoon sea salt, remaining 2 teaspoons extra-virgin olive oil, garlic, coriander, cumin, and green onions, stirring with a wooden spoon.

3 Add egg and ground turkey, and stir with the wooden spoon until combined.

4 Divide turkey into 8 small balls. Form each ball around a skewer to create 4-inch-long (10cm) kebabs. If using wooden skewers, soak skewers in water for at least 30 minutes beforehand. Set aside and wash hands with soap and water.

5 Thread remaining skewers with 3 tomatoes and 3 zucchini slices, alternately. (Make sure to keep raw turkey skewers and vegetable skewers on separate surfaces.)

6 Preheat the grill to medium-high. While waiting for the grill to heat, in a small bowl, whisk tahini, full-fat yogurt, lemon juice, and water. Add oregano and stir. Set aside.

7 When the grill is hot, cook kebabs about 3 minutes on each side, or until cooked through. Serve 2 vegetable and 2 turkey kebabs per person with a side of tahini yogurt.

Variation: If you don't have a grill at home, you can place skewers on a broiler pan and bake at 375°F (190°C) for 10 minutes. Turn kebabs and continue to cook for 10 to 15 minutes, or until cooked through.

EACH SERVING HAS:

| Calories 318 | Total Fat 19g | Carbohydrate 11g | Protein 28g |

Warmly spiced **chicken thighs** are seared golden brown; simmered alongside plump **apricots**, **green olives**, and **almonds**; and served over **cauliflower florets**.

Chicken Tagine with
Apricots and Green Olives

 6 CUPS   15 MINUTES   1 HOUR   2 CUPS

INGREDIENTS

- ½ tsp. ground cardamom
- ½ tsp. ground ginger
- ½ tsp. ground cinnamon
- ½ tsp. turmeric
- ¾ tsp. sea salt
- ¼ tsp. freshly ground black pepper
- ½ lb. (225g) boneless, skinless chicken thighs, diced
- 2 TB. extra-virgin olive oil
- ½ cup blanched almonds, coarsely chopped
- 4 garlic cloves, sliced
- ½ cup chicken stock
- ½ cup dried apricots, chopped
- ½ cup green olives, pitted
- 1 TB. preserved lemon rind, thinly sliced
- 1 medium head cauliflower, cut into florets
- ¼ cup fresh cilantro, chopped

METHOD

1 In a medium bowl, combine cardamom, ginger, cinnamon, turmeric, sea salt, and black pepper.

2 Place chicken thighs in the bowl and rub spice mixture on all sides. Save any extra spice mixture.

3 Heat a large Dutch oven or braiser over medium-high heat. When the Dutch oven is hot, add extra-virgin olive oil and wait 30 seconds.

4 Add diced chicken and cook for about 2 to 3 minutes, or until browned. Turn meat to brown all sides. Remove chicken from the Dutch oven and set aside.

5 Add almonds, garlic, and any residual spices to hot oil in the Dutch oven, and sauté, stirring constantly, for 30 seconds, or until lightly fragrant.

6 Add chicken stock to the hot Dutch oven and stir with a wooden spoon, scraping up any browned bits off the bottom.

7 Add apricots, green olives, and preserved lemon rind, and stir. Add cauliflower florets and gently stir again.

8 Place browned chicken on top. Cover and simmer for 45 to 50 minutes, or until chicken is cooked through.

9 Garnish warm chicken tagine with cilantro to serve.

EACH SERVING HAS:

| Calories 529 | Total Fat 33g | Carbohydrate 37g | Protein 30g |

Flavorful chicken thighs and **hearty vegetables** are robustly seasoned in a **classic Moroccan spice blend** for a sensational one-dish meal.

Moroccan Chicken

  4 THIGHS WITH VEGETABLES | **15 MINUTES** | **1 HOUR** | 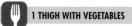 **1 THIGH WITH VEGETABLES**

INGREDIENTS

1 tsp. ground cumin

1 tsp. paprika

1 tsp. ground coriander

½ tsp. ground cinnamon

¼ tsp. cayenne pepper (optional)

1 tsp. sea salt

4 (4-oz.; 110g) skin-on chicken thighs

2 TB. extra-virgin olive oil

1 medium yellow onion, diced

2 garlic cloves, minced

1 medium carrot, minced

½ tsp. fresh ginger root, grated

3 medium zucchini, trimmed and cut into 1-in. (2.5cm) slices

2 medium tomatoes, diced

METHOD

1 Preheat the oven to 450°F (230°C). In a small bowl, combine cumin, paprika, coriander, cinnamon, cayenne pepper (if using), and sea salt.

2 Rub spice mixture on all sides of chicken thighs, making sure to get under and on top of skin.

3 Place a Dutch oven or large cast-iron skillet over medium-high heat. When the Dutch oven is hot, add 1 tablespoon extra-virgin olive oil and wait 30 seconds.

4 Place chicken, skin side down, in hot oil. Cook for 2 to 3 minutes, or until skins are nicely browned. Turn and repeat on other side. Remove chicken from the Dutch oven and set aside.

5 Add remaining 1 tablespoon extra-virgin olive oil to the hot Dutch oven. Add yellow onion, garlic, and carrot, and sauté, stirring frequently, for 2 to 3 minutes, or until onion is slightly translucent.

6 Add ginger root, zucchini, and tomatoes, and stir to combine. Remove from heat.

7 Place browned chicken, skin side down, on top of vegetables. Bake, uncovered, for 20 minutes. Remove from the oven. Carefully stir vegetables in the Dutch oven and turn chicken skin side up.

8 Return the Dutch oven to the oven and bake for 20 to 25 minutes, or until center of chicken reaches an internal temperature of 165°F (75°C).

9 Remove from the oven and serve chicken thighs alongside vegetables.

EACH SERVING HAS:

Calories **391**   Total Fat **27g**   Carbohydrate **17g**   Protein **23g**

Crisped petite game hens are rubbed in **fragrant ginger** and served with mellow roasted garlic and **toasted grapes.**

Ginger Game Hen with
Garlic and Grapes

 2 HENS   10 MINUTES   40 MINUTES   1 HEN

INGREDIENTS

½ lb. (225g) seedless red grapes

½ lb. (225g) seedless green grapes

10 small garlic cloves, peeled and halved

1 tsp. lemon zest or minced preserved lemon rind

2 TB. extra-virgin olive oil

1 cinnamon stick, broken in half

2 small Cornish game hens

1 tsp. ground ginger

1 tsp. sea salt

½ tsp. freshly ground black pepper

METHOD

1 Preheat the oven to 450°F (230°C).

2 In a large bowl, combine red grapes, green grapes, garlic, lemon zest, and extra-virgin olive oil, and toss until grapes are fully coated with oil.

3 Spread mixture evenly on a rimmed baking sheet or shallow baking dish. Place cinnamon stick halves among grapes.

4 Remove any giblets from inside of Cornish game hens. Pat skin dry with a paper towel.

5 Rub skin with ginger, sea salt, and black pepper. Place hens, breast side up, on top of grapes.

6 Bake for 30 to 40 minutes, or until hens reach a temperature of 165°F (75°C) in thickest part of breast or thigh.

7 Remove the baking sheet from the oven and discard cinnamon sticks. Serve roasted hens whole, alongside grapes and garlic.

If the Cornish game hens are getting too dark, place a piece of foil in a small tent over the birds. This will allow the meat to continue to cook without overbrowning the skin.

EACH SERVING HAS:

Calories **611**
Total Fat **30g**
Carbohydrate **65g**
Protein **28g**

Crisp **roast chicken breasts** are served with **garlic mashed sweet potatoes** and smothered in a **creamy leek sauce** with **fragrant thyme**.

Roast Chicken with
Creamy Leeks

 4 CHICKEN BREAST HALVES   **10 MINUTES**   **1 HOUR**   **1 CHICKEN BREAST HALF**

INGREDIENTS

2 medium sweet potatoes, peeled and quartered

4 to 6 whole garlic cloves, peeled

1½ cups chicken stock or broth

2 large chicken breasts, split, bone in and skin on

¾ tsp. sea salt

½ tsp. freshly ground black pepper

1 TB. unsalted butter or ghee (or use olive oil)

3 medium leeks, cleaned, trimmed, and sliced (white and light green parts only)

1 tsp. fresh thyme

1 tsp. Dijon mustard

¼ cup dry white wine

METHOD

1 Preheat the oven to 400°F (200°C).

2 Place sweet potatoes, garlic, and 1 cup chicken stock in a small ovenproof baking dish or casserole pan.

3 Place chicken breast halves, skin side up, on top of sweet potatoes. Sprinkle breasts with ½ teaspoon sea salt and ¼ teaspoon black pepper.

4 Bake chicken, uncovered, for 45 to 60 minutes, or until it reaches an internal temperature of 165°F (75°C).

5 About 15 minutes before chicken is done, place a medium skillet over medium-high heat.

6 When the skillet is hot, add unsalted butter, leeks, remaining ¼ teaspoon sea salt (if desired), remaining ¼ teaspoon black pepper, and thyme. Sauté, stirring frequently, for 4 to 6 minutes, or until leeks are soft.

7 Add Dijon mustard, dry white wine, and remaining ½ cup chicken stock. Cover and simmer until chicken is finished cooking.

8 When chicken is done, set aside to rest for 5 minutes. Transfer sweet potatoes, garlic, and remaining pan juices to a food processor, and purée until mashed.

9 Cut each chicken breast into slices. Serve with creamy leeks on top of mashed sweet potatoes.

EACH SERVING HAS:

Calories **409**   Total Fat **13g**   Carbohydrate **28g**   Protein **39g**

beef, pork, and lamb

This chapter provides a few great recipes for beef, pork, and lamb—meats that are a part of the Mediterranean Paleo diet, but aren't encouraged daily. From simple Beef Kofta to extravagant Pork Loin Roulade, these recipes showcase these flavorful meats.

If you can find an alternative grass-fed or pasture-raised option—such as elk, bison, or venison—you can always substitute these similar cuts into the recipes.

CORIANDER-CRUSTED BEEF

 1 ROAST   **1 HOUR**   **4 HOURS, 10 MINUTES**   **1/10 ROAST**

INGREDIENTS

5-lb. (2.25kg) beef chuck or shoulder roast

1/4 cup whole coriander seeds, crushed

1 TB. sea salt

1 tsp. freshly ground black pepper

3 TB. extra-virgin olive oil

1 large yellow onion, diced

5 garlic cloves, crushed

1 cup beef stock or broth, or water

5 medium carrots, trimmed and cut into 1-in. (2.5cm) slices

1 celery root, peeled and diced into 1-in. (2.5cm) cubes

METHOD

1 Season beef chuck roast on all sides with coriander, sea salt, and black pepper. Let roast sit at room temperature for 30 minutes.

2 Preheat the oven to 275°F (140°C).

3 Heat a large Dutch oven or heavy-bottomed pot over high heat. When the Dutch oven is hot, add 2 tablespoons extra-virgin olive oil and wait 30 seconds.

4 Place roast in hot oil for 2 to 3 minutes, or until a deep golden crust forms. Turn roast and repeat to brown all sides. Remove roast from the Dutch oven.

5 Add remaining 1 tablespoon extra-virgin olive oil to the hot Dutch oven. Add yellow onion and garlic, and sauté, stirring frequently, for 2 to 3 minutes, or until onion is slightly translucent.

6 Add beef stock and stir with a wooden spoon to remove any browned bits from the bottom of the Dutch oven. Remove from heat.

7 Add carrots and celery root, and place browned roast on top of vegetables. Cover and bake for 4 hours, or until beef is tender. Serve with Olive-Nut Tapenade.

EACH SERVING HAS:

Calories **422**   Total Fat **22g**   Carbohydrate **10g**   Protein **46g**

OLIVE-NUT TAPENADE

 2 CUPS   **10 MINUTES**   **NONE**   **1/4 CUP**

INGREDIENTS

1 1/2 cups green olives, pitted and chopped

1/2 cup raw nuts of choice, chopped

1 garlic clove, minced

1 tsp. whole-grain mustard

1/4 cup fresh cilantro, chopped

1/2 cup extra-virgin olive oil

2 tsp. sherry vinegar or red wine vinegar

METHOD

1 In a medium nonmetal bowl, place green olives, raw nuts, garlic, whole-grain mustard, cilantro, extra-virgin olive oil, and sherry vinegar. Stir with a fork until fully combined. Alternately, place ingredients into a food processor and pulse until a rough paste forms.

2 Serve tapenade on top of sliced Coriander-Crusted Beef and vegetables.

EACH SERVING HAS:

Calories **140**   Total Fat **14g**   Carbohydrate **4g**   Protein **1g**

Tender roast beef and vegetables are slow cooked with whole coriander and served with a vibrant tapenade of olive, nuts, cilantro, and sherry vinegar.

Coriander-Crusted Beef
with Olive-Nut Tapenade

Warmly spiced beef kebabs with **crunchy pine nuts** and **tart sumac**—the perfect protein to serve alongside **fresh greens** or **steamed vegetables.**

Beef Kofta with Pine Nuts and Sumac

 8 KOFTA   10 MINUTES   6 MINUTES   2 KOFTA

INGREDIENTS

- 1 lb. (450g) lean ground beef
- ½ medium yellow onion, finely diced or grated
- ¼ cup toasted pine nuts, coarsely chopped
- 2 TB. fresh parsley, minced
- 1 tsp. ground cumin
- 1 tsp. sumac
- ½ tsp. ground cinnamon
- ¼ tsp. cayenne pepper
- 1 tsp. sea salt
- ¼ tsp. freshly ground black pepper

METHOD

1 In a large bowl, thoroughly mix ground beef, yellow onion, toasted pine nuts, parsley, cumin, sumac, cinnamon, cayenne pepper, sea salt, and black pepper.

2 Shape into 8 small balls. Mold 1 ball around each skewer (if using wooden skewers, soak in water for at least 30 minutes beforehand).

3 Preheat the grill to medium-high. When the grill is hot, cook kofta for about 3 minutes on each side, or until cooked through.

4 Serve warm with tzatziki, hummus, tapenade, zhug, tahini, or flatbread; eat them on their own as a snack; or have them as a breakfast or salad protein.

Variation: If you don't have a grill at home, you can still easily make these skewers as small "meatballs" instead. Skip the skewers and sauté in a bit of extra-virgin olive oil over medium high-heat for 3 to 5 minutes on each side, or until cooked through.

Kofta refers to any kebab made with ground meat in place of cubed meat. Instead of marinating the meat to get extra flavor, the spices are mixed right in. Feel free to use any kind of unseasoned ground meat in this recipe. Lamb, bison, and dark-meat chicken are excellent choices.

EACH SERVING HAS:

Calories **216**   Total Fat **12g**   Carbohydrate **3g**   Protein **26g**

This extra-fancy dish—with **pounded pork loin** rolled in **figs, almonds,** and **fresh sage**—is great for holidays and special occasions.

Pork Loin Roulade with
Figs and Almonds

 1 LOIN   **25 MINUTES**   **2 HOURS**   **⅙ LOIN**

INGREDIENTS

3 lb. (1.5kg) boneless pork loin

1½ tsp. sea salt

1 tsp. freshly ground black pepper

2 TB. extra-virgin olive oil

¾ cup yellow onion, diced

¼ cup fresh sage leaves, chopped

¼ cup slivered almonds, coarsely chopped

½ cup dried figs, stems removed and coarsely chopped

1 tsp. sherry vinegar

4 lb. (2kg) delicata squash, trimmed, seeded, and sliced (or use peeled and sliced butternut squash)

1¼ cups vegetable or chicken stock

EACH SERVING HAS:

Calories 521
Total Fat 25g
Carbohydrate 22g
Protein 51g

METHOD

1 Preheat the oven to 350°F (180°C).

2 Place pork loin on a cutting board. Using a sharp knife, butterfly loin by slicing parallel to the cutting board from right to left. Stop just short of the opposite edge, so flap stays attached by a ¼-inch (.5cm) section.

3 Open sliced loin flat, and place between two sheets of plastic wrap on a sturdy surface. Using a meat tenderizer, pound loin to ½- to ¾-inch (1.25 to 2cm) thickness. Remove the plastic wrap and sprinkle pork with sea salt and black pepper.

4 Place a medium skillet over medium-high heat. When the skillet is hot, add extra-virgin olive oil and wait 30 seconds.

5 Add yellow onion and sauté, stirring frequently, for 3 to 5 minutes, or until onion is translucent.

6 Add sage, almonds, figs, and sherry vinegar, and cook, stirring occasionally, for 3 to 4 minutes, or until figs soften. Using a wooden spoon, spread mixture on loin.

7 Starting on one end, roll loin into a roulade. Using nondyed cooking twine, firmly tie center of roulade together. Moving out to edge, tie pieces of twine every 1 inch (2.5cm).

8 Place delicata squash and vegetable stock in a Dutch oven. Place roulade on top of squash.

9 Cover and bake, basting every 30 minutes, for 1 hour, 15 minutes, or until pork reaches an internal temperature of 115°F (45°C). Remove the lid and bake for 30 minutes, or until pork reaches an internal temperature of 145°F (65°C).

10 Remove the twine. Slice roulade and serve over squash.

Spicy **Spanish chorizo** is simmered in **apple cider** with **fresh bell peppers** and sweet yellow onions.

Chorizo in Sidra (Cider)

 4 CUPS   10 MINUTES   55 MINUTES   1 CUP

INGREDIENTS

1 TB. extra-virgin olive oil

1 large yellow onion, diced

2 large green bell peppers, seeded and diced

1 lb. (450g) fresh Spanish chorizo, sliced into 1-in. (2.5cm) pieces

3 cups nonalcoholic apple cider

2 thyme sprigs

1 garlic clove, crushed

METHOD

1 Place a medium Dutch oven or braiser over medium-high heat. When the Dutch oven is hot, add extra-virgin olive oil and wait 30 seconds.

2 Add yellow onion and sauté, stirring frequently, for 3 to 5 minutes, or until slightly translucent.

3 Add green bell peppers and cook, stirring occasionally, for 2 to 3 minutes, or until slightly softened.

4 Add Spanish chorizo, nonalcoholic apple cider, thyme, and garlic. Simmer, uncovered, for 30 to 45 minutes, or until cider has reduced by half.

5 Remove thyme and garlic clove before serving chorizo.

There are many different kinds of sausage called *chorizo*. This recipe specifically calls for hard Spanish chorizo in casings. If you can't find this variety, however, you may substitute any fresh garlic sausage.

EACH SERVING HAS:

Calories **512**   Total Fat **34g**   Carbohydrate **23g**   Protein **29g**

Succulent lamb chops are smothered in a **sweet pomegranate, honey,** and rosemary–infused glaze.

Lamb Chops with
Pomegranate Glaze

 8 CHOPS 40 MINUTES 30 MINUTES 2 CHOPS

INGREDIENTS

8 small bone-in lamb chops

1 tsp. sea salt

½ tsp. freshly ground black pepper

1 cup pure pomegranate juice

2 TB. raw honey

2 TB. fresh orange juice

2 tsp. cognac or balsamic vinegar (optional)

1 sprig fresh rosemary

1 TB. extra-virgin olive oil

METHOD

1 Season lamb chops on both sides with sea salt and black pepper. Leave out at room temperature for 30 minutes.

2 In a small saucepan, stir together pomegranate juice, raw honey, orange juice, and cognac (if using), and place over medium heat. Place rosemary sprig in the pan.

3 Bring to a simmer, stirring occasionally, for 18 to 20 minutes, or until reduced to a syruplike consistency (glaze will continue to thicken as it cools). Remove from heat and discard rosemary sprig.

4 Heat a large skillet over medium-high heat. When the skillet is hot, add extra-virgin olive oil and wait 30 seconds.

5 Place seasoned lamb chops in the hot skillet and cook for 3 to 4 minutes per side, or until cooked to desired temperature.

6 Brush with pomegranate glaze to serve.

EACH SERVING HAS:

Calories **436**   Total Fat **8g**   Carbohydrate **31g**   Protein **30g**

This traditional Moroccan **sweet-and-savory stew** features **warmly spiced lamb** simmered until tender, with **almonds, prunes, apricots,** and **cauliflower.**

Lamb and Prune Tagine

 8 CUPS   **20 MINUTES**   **1 HOUR, 10 MINUTES**   **2 CUPS**

INGREDIENTS

2 TB. extra-virgin olive oil

2-lb. (1kg) lamb shoulder

½ cup blanched slivered almonds

1 medium yellow onion, diced

3 garlic cloves, sliced

1 tsp. sea salt

1 tsp. ground ginger

1 tsp. ground coriander

1 tsp. turmeric

2 cups hot water

2 cinnamon sticks

1 large head cauliflower, cut into florets

¼ cup prunes, pitted and quartered

¼ cup dried apricots, sliced

4 whole cloves

1 TB. honey

1 TB. orange blossom water (optional)

¼ tsp. freshly ground nutmeg

¼ cup cilantro, chopped

METHOD

1 Heat a large Dutch oven or braiser over medium-high heat. When the Dutch oven is hot, add extra-virgin olive oil and wait 30 seconds.

2 Add lamb shoulder and sear, stirring frequently, for 3 to 4 minutes, or until browned on all sides. Remove from the Dutch oven and set aside.

3 Add almonds to hot oil in the Dutch oven and sauté, stirring constantly, for 30 seconds, or until lightly golden. Add yellow onion, garlic, and sea salt, and continue to cook, stirring frequently, for 1 to 2 minutes, or until slightly translucent.

4 Add ginger, coriander, and turmeric, and sauté for 30 seconds, or until highly fragrant.

5 Add browned lamb, hot water, and cinnamon sticks. Stir, cover, and simmer for 45 minutes.

6 Meanwhile, place cauliflower florets into a food processor. Pulse for 15 seconds, or until a ricelike consistency is achieved.

7 After 45 minutes, add prunes, apricots, cloves, honey, orange blossom water (if using), nutmeg, and cauliflower rice to the Dutch oven. Cover and cook for an additional 20 minutes, or until lamb is tender. Garnish with cilantro to serve.

EACH SERVING HAS:

Calories **676**

Total Fat **34g**

Carbohydrate **41g**

Protein **57g**

Rich lamb and robust vegetable skewers are grilled to perfection and served atop a chilled cucumber and mint salad with za'atar.

Marinated Lamb Kebabs
with Cucumber-Mint Salad

MARINATED LAMB KEBABS

 5 KEBABS   **1 HOUR**   **8 MINUTES**   **1 KEBAB**

INGREDIENTS

2 TB. extra-virgin olive oil

1 tsp. red wine vinegar

3 garlic cloves, minced

2 TB. fresh rosemary, finely chopped

1 tsp. coriander seeds, crushed

¾ tsp. sea salt

¼ tsp. crushed red pepper flakes

1 lb. (450g) boneless leg of lamb, cut into 1¼-in. (3cm) cubes

1 medium red onion, cut into 1¼-in. (3cm) squares

2 medium red bell peppers, cleaned and cut into 1¼-in. (3cm) squares

1 medium zucchini, cut into ½-in. (1.25cm) slices

METHOD

1 In a shallow dish that's long enough to hold skewers, mix extra-virgin olive oil, red wine vinegar, garlic, rosemary, coriander, sea salt, and crushed red pepper flakes.

2 Carefully thread lamb cubes, red onion, red bell peppers, and zucchini evenly onto 8 skewers. Place skewers in marinade and turn each to be sure marinade covers all sides. Cover and refrigerate for 30 minutes to 1 hour, turning skewers in marinade once or twice, if possible.

3 Shortly before mealtime, heat the grill to medium-high. Remove kebabs from marinade and discard leftover liquid. Grill kebabs for 3 to 4 minutes. Turn over, and continue to grill for 3 to 4 minutes, or until lamb is cooked as desired.

4 Serve kebabs over chilled Cucumber-Mint Salad.

EACH SERVING HAS:

Calories 283

Total Fat 21g

Carbohydrate 9g

Protein 18g

CUCUMBER-MINT SALAD

 4 CUPS   **40 MINUTES**   **NONE**   **1 CUP**

INGREDIENTS

2 medium English cucumbers, halved and thinly sliced

¼ red onion, thinly sliced

6 TB. fresh mint, chopped

Juice of ½ medium lemon (about 1 TB.)

2 TB. extra-virgin olive oil

2 tsp. za'atar

METHOD

1 In a large bowl, toss English cucumbers, red onion, mint, lemon juice, extra-virgin olive oil, and za'atar until vegetables are fully coated.

2 Chill for 30 minutes before serving under Marinated Lamb Kebabs.

EACH SERVING HAS:

Calories 97   Total Fat 7g   Carbohydrate 10g   Protein 3g

desserts

While desserts shouldn't be the primary focus of the Mediterranean Paleo diet, they sure are a delicious indulgence. These recipes use raw honey, coconut sugar, or naturally sweet ripe fruits to add a tasty treat to your diet every once in a while. There's really no substitute for fresh, sun-ripened fruits, so always remember to use what's in season for the most satisfying sweets.

Crackling coconut sugar is caramelized to dark amber on **glistening orange, grapefruit,** and **lemon slices.**

Citrus Brûlée

 12 SLICES   5 MINUTES   8 MINUTES   2 SLICES

INGREDIENTS

1 medium orange

1 medium pink grapefruit

1 lemon or lime

½ tsp. ground ginger

¼ cup coconut sugar

METHOD

1 Arrange the oven rack to the highest position. Preheat the broiler to high.

2 Slice orange, pink grapefruit, and lemon into ½-inch (1.25cm) slices, discarding end pieces of peel and any seeds.

3 Line a rimmed baking sheet with aluminum foil. Spread citrus slices evenly on the foil-lined baking sheet.

4 Sprinkle each slice with a small pinch of ginger. Next, sprinkle 1 to 2 teaspoons coconut sugar on each slice.

5 Place the baking sheet on the highest oven rack and broil for 6 to 8 minutes, or until sugar caramelizes and turns a dark amber color. Remove from the oven immediately. Note: Be sure to watch constantly during the last few minutes. It takes only a few seconds to go from amber to burnt.

6 Cool citrus slices before serving. Don't eat rinds.

Variation: To make **Orange Blossom Brûlée,** use orange slices sprinkled with a touch of orange blossom water instead of ginger. Sprinkle with coconut sugar and broil as described.

Use any citrus you can find for this simple dessert. Try Meyer lemons, Key limes, tangelos, mandarins, or blood oranges. Just remember that lemons and limes are so tart they need extra coconut sugar; for variety, you can also pair them with sweeter citrus.

EACH SERVING HAS:

Calories 72
Total Fat 0g
Carbohydrate 19g
Protein 1g

Rich dark chocolate coated in **crumbly hazelnuts** surrounds **luscious fresh figs** for a decadent treat.

Chocolate-Covered Figs with Hazelnuts

 12 FIGS   1 TO 2 HOURS   15 MINUTES   2 FIGS

INGREDIENTS

12 fresh figs

8 oz. (225g) dark or bittersweet chocolate chips (at least 60 percent cacao)

½ cup toasted hazelnuts, chopped

METHOD

1 Cut a square or rectangle of parchment paper to line the bottom of a small metal baking sheet or cake pan.

2 Carefully rinse figs, and pat dry with a paper towel.

3 Place a small heavy-bottomed saucepan or double boiler over medium-low heat. A double boiler is best, or you can make one with a metal bowl that fits over a saucepan with about 2 inches (5cm) of space between the bottom of the bowl and the bottom of the pan. Make sure to add 1 inch (2.5cm) of water to the bottom pan before heating.

4 Add dark chocolate chips to the saucepan and stir for 10 to 15 minutes, or until completely melted. Remove from heat.

5 Make sure figs are completely dry. Holding each fig by the stem, dip into melted chocolate, and sprinkle with chopped hazelnuts. Place on the parchment paper.

6 Place the baking sheet with figs in the refrigerator for 1 to 2 hours, or until chocolate hardens. Serve chilled.

Variation: In place of figs, use fresh ripe strawberries, cherries, or whatever fruit is sweet and in season to make this recipe year-round. Or use soft pitted prunes or dried apricots for a winter variety.

EACH SERVING HAS:

Calories 336   Total Fat 21g   Carbohydrate 41g   Protein 5g

This **delicate almond cake** is simple and delicious. Flavored with **almond extract** and **raw honey,** it's sure to please even the pickiest Paleo eaters.

Olive Oil **Almond Cake**

 1 CAKE　　 **10 MINUTES**　　 **50 MINUTES**　　 **¹⁄₁₀ CAKE**

INGREDIENTS

2 cups almond flour

¾ cup tapioca flour

¼ tsp. sea salt

½ tsp. baking soda

½ cup extra-virgin olive oil

¾ cup raw honey

4 large eggs

½ cup coconut milk or heavy cream

1½ tsp. almond extract

1 tsp. lemon juice

¼ cup sliced almonds, toasted

METHOD

1 Preheat the oven to 350°F (180°C).

2 In a large bowl, stir together almond flour, tapioca flour, sea salt, and baking soda with a fork until fully blended.

3 In a medium bowl, whisk together extra-virgin olive oil, ½ cup raw honey, eggs, coconut milk, and almond extract until fully blended. Add lemon juice and whisk again.

4 Pour liquid batter into dry mixture and stir with a wooden spoon until fully incorporated.

5 Lightly grease a silicone Bundt pan with extra-virgin olive oil. Alternately, use a 9-inch (23cm) round cake pan; however, a Bundt pan works best. If using a silicone pan, place on a sturdy metal baking sheet. If using a round cake pan, line the greased pan with a 9-inch (23cm) circle of parchment paper.

6 Pour batter into the pan and let sit for 5 minutes.

7 Place the pan (on the baking sheet, if silicone) in the oven and bake for 40 to 50 minutes, or until a toothpick inserted into cake comes out clean.

8 Let cool completely. Invert the pan over a serving plate and gently remove the pan from cake.

9 Drizzle with remaining ¼ cup raw honey and sprinkle with toasted almonds to serve.

EACH SERVING HAS:

| Calories 386 | Total Fat 27g | Carbohydrate 73g | Protein 8g |

Ripe pears are simmered in **sticky-sweet Pedro Ximénez sherry** with **fragrant vanilla** and **cloves**.

Pears Poached in Sherry

 2 PEARS   5 MINUTES   30 MINUTES   ½ PEAR

INGREDIENTS

2 medium firm pears

½ fresh vanilla bean

2 cups Pedro Ximénez sherry

2 whole cloves

METHOD

1 Using a small paring knife or vegetable peeler, peel pears. Slice each pear in half from stem to blossom end. Using a melon baller or a sturdy metal spoon, remove core and seeds from each half.

2 Cut vanilla bean in half lengthwise. Using the back of the knife (the dull side), scrape out seeds. Reserve seeds and discard pods.

3 In a small saucepan over medium-high heat, pour Pedro Ximénez sherry. Add vanilla bean seeds and cloves, and stir.

4 When sherry begins to simmer, add pear halves and cook, turning occasionally, for 8 to 12 minutes, or until pears are tender but not mushy.

5 Using a slotted spoon, remove pear halves from liquid and place each in a serving bowl to cool.

6 Remove sherry mixture from heat, and discard cloves. Drizzle a few spoonfuls of sherry mixture over each pear to serve.

Pedro Ximénez sherry, also known as P.X. sherry, is a sweet fermented wine made from late-harvested or sun-dried grapes, making the final product high in natural sugars. Use this sticky-sweet sherry for special occasions, or in limited quantities, as it's very high in carbohydrates.

EACH SERVING HAS:

Calories 140

Total Fat 0g

Carbohydrate 21g

Protein 1g

This **simple Sicilian iced dessert,** with **fresh strawberries** and **cooling mint tea,** is a refreshing summertime treat.

Strawberry-Mint Granita

 2½ CUPS   4 HOURS, 45 MINUTES   NONE   ½ CUP

INGREDIENTS

2 cups fresh strawberries, sliced and with greens removed

1 cup steeped mint tea, cooled

2 TB. raw honey

METHOD

1 In a blender, combine strawberries, mint tea, and raw honey. Pulse to form a purée.

2 Spread mixture evenly in an 8-inch (20cm) square baking dish. Place in the freezer for 30 minutes.

3 Stir mixture thoroughly with a metal fork, and spread evenly in the dish again. Repeat every 30 minutes for 3 to 4 hours.

4 Stir again before serving. Granita will hold for up to 12 hours.

Variation: To make **Cantaloupe-Mint Granita,** simply replace strawberries with 2 cups chopped cantaloupe. Substitute any fresh, ripe fruit for an endless variety of granita flavors.

> Making homemade mint tea is easy with fresh mint. Simply pour 1 cup just-boiled water over 8 to 10 fresh mint leaves. Let steep for 10 to 15 minutes, and then remove mint leaves.

EACH SERVING HAS:

Calories **45**   Total Fat **0g**   Carbohydrate **11g**   Protein **0g**

Soft, sweet, and delicious, these **honey-caramelized peaches** are covered in **crunchy pistachios** and scented with **fragrant orange blossom water.**

Roasted Peaches with Nuts and Honey

 3 CUPS 10 MINUTES 20 MINUTES ½ CUP

INGREDIENTS

3 ripe peaches, pitted and halved

1 tsp. extra-virgin olive oil

2 tsp. raw honey

2 TB. pistachios, coarsely chopped

½ tsp. orange blossom water (optional)

⅛ tsp. sea salt (optional)

METHOD

1 Preheat the oven to 400°F (200°C). Adjust the oven racks to the highest setting that will still allow for the baking sheet.

2 Slice each peach half into 4 slices. Place peaches on a rimmed metal baking sheet and drizzle with extra-virgin olive oil.

3 Bake for 10 minutes. Gently stir peaches with a wooden spoon, and bake for 5 minutes, or until softened.

4 Remove peaches from the oven, and turn the broiler on high. Drizzle peaches with raw honey and sprinkle with pistachios.

5 Broil peaches for 1 to 3 minutes, or until deeply browned and caramelized on top. Watch carefully so peaches don't burn.

6 Right before serving, sprinkle with orange blossom water (if using) and sea salt (if using).

Variation: To make **Roasted Apricots with Pecans,** substitute 6 fresh apricots, quartered, instead of peaches, and use 2 tablespoons chopped pecans instead of pistachios.

EACH SERVING HAS:

Calories **53**   Total Fat **1g**   Carbohydrate **11g**   Protein **1g**

Intensely dark chocolate cake, dense and chewy, is sprinkled with a dusting of smoked paprika.

Dark Chocolate Paprika Cake

 1 CAKE   15 MINUTES   1 HOUR, 5 MINUTES   ¹⁄₁₆ CAKE

INGREDIENTS

1 cup unsalted butter, cut up

¼ cup heavy cream

8 oz. (225g) bittersweet chocolate (at least 60 percent cacao), chopped

5 large eggs

1 cup coconut sugar

¼ cup unsweetened cocoa powder

1 tsp. smoked paprika

METHOD

1 Preheat the oven to 350°F (180°C).

2 Lightly grease a silicone Bundt pan with extra-virgin olive oil. Alternately, use a 9-inch (23cm) round cake pan; however, a Bundt pan works best. If using a silicone pan, place on a sturdy metal baking sheet. If using a round cake pan, line a greased pan with a 9-inch (23cm) circle of parchment paper.

3 In a small saucepan over medium-low heat, combine unsalted butter and heavy cream. When butter is melted, add bittersweet chocolate and stir constantly for about 10 to 15 minutes, or until melted. Remove from heat.

4 In a medium bowl, beat eggs, coconut sugar, and unsweetened cocoa powder. Slowly drizzle in chocolate mixture, and whisk until fully combined.

5 Pour batter into the greased pan. Sprinkle with smoked paprika and let sit for 5 minutes.

6 Place the pan (on the baking sheet, if silicone) in the oven and bake for 40 to 50 minutes, or until a toothpick inserted into cake comes out clean.

7 Remove cake from the oven and let cool completely. Invert pan over a serving plate and gently remove the pan from cake. Slice before serving.

EACH SERVING HAS:

| Calories 255 | Total Fat 20g | Carbohydrate 21g | Protein 3g |

Chewy apricots and **scented orange blossom water** flavor these delicious no-bake **Paleo** "cookies."

Apricot Macadamia
Balls

 16 BALLS    **1 HOUR, 5 MINUTES**   **NONE**   **4 BALLS**

INGREDIENTS

½ cup dried apricots, finely chopped

1 tsp. fresh orange zest

½ tsp. ground cardamom

1 tsp. raw honey

1 tsp. orange blossom water

2 cups raw macadamia nuts

METHOD

1 In a small bowl, combine dried apricots, orange zest, cardamom, and raw honey. Sprinkle with orange blossom water and set aside.

2 In a food processor, place macadamia nuts and pulse until a cookie dough consistency forms.

3 Transfer apricot mixture into the food processor and pulse a few more times to fully blend dough.

4 Shape dough into 1-inch (2.5cm) balls and place on a parchment-lined baking sheet.

5 Place the baking sheet in the refrigerator and chill at least 1 hour, or until firm. Serve cold.

> These tasty treats are the perfect snack to curb any sweet craving. They can also be made ahead of time and kept in the freezer for up to 2 months for desserts on the go.

EACH SERVING HAS:

Calories	Total Fat	Carbohydrate	Protein
149	11g	13g	2g

Index

Photo Credits

Page 10
Steve Gorton © Dorling Kindersley
Dave King © Dorling Kindersley
Simon Smith © Dorling Kindersley
Philip Dowell © Dorling Kindersley
Gerard Brown © Dorling Kindersley

Page 11
Steve Gorton © Dorling Kindersley
Roger Dixon © Dorling Kindersley
Will Heap © Dorling Kindersley
Stephen Oliver © Dorling Kindersley

Page 14
Philip Dowell © Dorling Kindersley
Dave King © Dorling Kindersley
Will Heap © Dorling Kindersley
Steve Gorton © Dorling Kindersley
Roger Dixon © Dorling Kindersley
Gerard Brown © Dorling Kindersley

Page 15
Dave King © Dorling Kindersley
Geoff Dann © Dorling Kindersley
William Reavell © Dorling Kindersley

Page 16-17
Emma Firth © Dorling Kindersley

Page 22
Roger Dixon © Dorling Kindersley
Ian O'Leary © Dorling Kindersley
Philip Dowell © Dorling Kindersley
John Whittaker © Dorling Kindersley

Page 23
Charlotte Tolhurst © Dorling Kindersley
David Murray © Dorling Kindersley
Roger Dixon © Dorling Kindersley